THE U... 1000 SINGLES
2ND EDITION

PAUL GAMBACCINI · JONATHAN RICE · TIM RICE

**Editorial Associate
TONY BROWN**

GUINNESS PUBLISHING

ACKNOWLEDGEMENTS

The photographs in this edition were supplied by Pictorial Press, London Features International, Popperfoto and Mono Music AB.

Editor: David Roberts
Deputy Editor: Paola Simoneschi
Typesetting and Layout: Sallie Collins

© GRR Publications Ltd 1993

First edition 1988

Published in Great Britain by Guinness Publishing Ltd, 33 London Road, Enfield, Middlesex, EN2 6DJ.

Printed and bound in Great Britain by The Bath Press.

A catalogue record for this book is available from The British Library.

ISBN 0-85112-712-6

INTRODUCTION

PART 1: THE UK TOP 1000 SINGLES

A listing of the Top 1000 Hits, in ranking order, from 'Rock Around The Clock' in 1955 to 16 May 1993.

PART 2: THE YEAR BY YEAR TOP 40 CHARTS

A ranking of the Top 40 hits for each year.

PART 3: THE ARTISTS

An alphabetical listing of the artists who made the Top 1000 hits.

THE GUINNESS BOOK OF BRITISH HIT SINGLES, now a million-seller and in its 9th edition, contains 4261 chart acts and 17296 hits. Illustrated with 200 new pictures, this 432-page book is *the* bible for rock and pop fans. ISBN 0-85112-526-3

THE GUINNESS BOOK OF TOP 40 CHARTS presents popular music's life line through the years. The 700+ pages feature every chart for every week dating back to 10 March 1960, plus a detailed year-by-year breakdown of the smaller charts from the 1950s.

If you ever wanted to know what the hits were on your birthday, *The Guinness Book of Top 40 Charts* will reveal all and there is so much more to discover:

What single was at the top of the charts the week the Beatles first hit the Top 40?

Was the summer of '67 all legend has made it out to be? Who were the artists the Sex Pistols were shaking up when they first poked their gobs into the Top 40 in late 1976?

These questions and a host of others are answered in *The Guinness Book of Top 40 Charts*. ISBN 0-85112-541-7

THE GUINNESS BOOK OF BRITISH HIT ALBUMS is now in its fifth edition and lists every recording to have made the album chart since it began in 1958.

Illustrated with 100 photographs and running to 400+ fact-filled pages, the latest edition is bigger and offers more value for money than ever.
ISBN 0-85112-527-1

THE GUINNESS HITS QUIZ 2 contains brain-bursting quizzes, anagrams and acrostics covering the whole of the popular music scene. Ideal for journeys and get togethers – and indispensible for the pub quiz – *The Guinness Hits Quiz 2* was described by Q magazine as a book where '*the compilers really know their stuff and, as a result, there is something for everyone*'.
ISBN 0-85112-712-6

They do write them like they used to. At a time when the decline of the single and the demise of popular music itself are being proclaimed by culture commentators who confuse change with death, mass appeal records are as successful as ever. Indeed, because of the recently diminished number of singles with traditional song structures, those that do cross the boundaries of the currently fragmented music audiences are likely to enjoy greater chart domination than at any point in history.

The proof is in this second edition of *UK Top 1000 Singles*. The top three tunes, measured in terms of chart performance, were all number one in the period 1991-92. For a single two-year period to dominate an all-time list like that is more than coincidence. Our first edition, which covered the period 1955-88, honoured three discs with nine weeks each at number one as our all-time winners. They have all been swept aside.

The new number one is '(Everything I Do) I Do It For You' by Bryan Adams. This song from the film *Robin Hood: Prince Of Thieves* assumed the top spot the week of 13 July 1991 and held it for a total of 16 consecutive weeks. Only 'I Believe' by Frankie Laine from 1953, a pre-rock era year not included in this volume, had ever been number one for longer, and it took that hit three different runs at the top to accumulate 18 weeks. Proving such a long-running chart topper was not a fluke was 'I Will Always Love You' by Whitney Houston, oddly enough from another Kevin Costner movie, *The Bodyguard*. This interpretation of a Dolly Parton song commanded the field for ten weeks in late 1992 and early 1993, taking the all-time number three position.

We say number three instead of two because in between the two movie marvels 'Bohemian Rhapsody' by Queen returned to the number one position. Number one for nine weeks on its original release in 1975, its five-week run following the death of lead singer Freddie Mercury gave it a distinction unlikely to be equalled: it has been number one in four different calendar years, twice being a Christmas number one that held over into the New Year.

Even this all-change in the top three doesn't tell the complete story of how the big chart hits have been bigger since our first edition. There were 93 number ones between 'I Just Called To Say I Love You' by Stevie Wonder in 1984 and 'Ride On Time' by Black Box five years later, none of which remained at the top for more than five weeks. 'Ride On Time' lasted for six, beginning the recent era of long-running number ones. 'Stay' by Shakespears Sister, an eight-week champ, and 'Rhythm Is A Dancer' by Snap!, a six-week star, have also moved into our Top 1000 in the top 50. As with the late 1950s before it, the early 1990s are now disproportionately represented in the upper regions of the chart. Singles sales are generally down, but to the benefit of number ones, which are enjoying bigger sales leads over number twos and longer runs at the top. 1992 tied with 1962 as the year with the fewest number of new chart toppers, 12. It was also the first year since 1971 in which no number one stayed in front for only one week. The lesson to any act which cares to take it is that although specialised audiences are demanding esoteric material, the general public still hungers for singles with a more or less traditional song structure. New styles like rap, as in 'Rhythm Is A Dancer', or sampling, as in 'Ride On Time', can be incorporated, but the mass audience desperately wants to be able to remember a tune and relate to a lyric.

In this book we rate the hits according to weeks spent at number one. When a tie occurs we compare weeks at number two. If there is still a tie we refer to weeks at three and so forth down the chart until all ties are broken. After we have ordered all the number ones we go on to the singles that peaked at two. There have been more than enough of these to fill the top 1000. It will interest many readers to know that the lowest point to which we had to refer to break a tie was 26. The year listed in our chart for each single is, in all cases, the first year of top five chart entry.

In the pages herein we list our top 1000 of the rock era. Next to a title we give the number of weeks the disc spent at each of the top five positions. When these figures are the same, be assured that the tie was broken by reference to a lower position. No two records in our top 1000 had identical chart histories.

We begin our computations with 'Rock Around The Clock', the first rock 'n' roll number one, even though the British charts began in 1952. Prior to Bill Haley's hit, singles moved much more slowly up and down the top ten, and to include these early successes would incline the top 1000 in favour of the early and mid-50s. For such a short era to dominate the all-time totals would be inequitable, so we have omitted the pre-rock chart period from November 1952 to November 1955. With a tip of the hat to artists who achieved at that time we acknowledge that, in chart terms, this three-year period was an era unto itself. The charts we have consulted for our listing are the same we use for *British Hit Singles*: the *New Musical Express* until the end of February 1960 and *Record Retailer* (which became *Music Week*) from the beginning of March of that year.

When looking at our top 1000 please remember that this is not a sales chart. Although the weekly chart always ranks singles in order of sales, the total volume of purchase changes every week and is subject to seasonal fluctuations. A number one record on chart will most likely sell a different amount of copies from the leader the weeks before and after. Merely comparing charts cannot provide clues to total sales. Indeed, it is almost certainly impossible to compile an accurate top 1000 based on sales, since many labels no longer exist and some that still do either did not keep strictly precise figures or are reluctant to release them. The very best sellers are, of course, widely known. The famine relief record 'Do They Know It's Christmas' sold over three million copies during the 1984 Christmas period to become Britain's all-time best-selling single.

Here it is, our ranking of the biggest UK hits of the rock era based on highest chart positions reached and sustained. Our special congratulations go to those artists who have appeared in the top 1000 for the first time since our first edition in 1988. Our condolences go to the makers of the 139 entries from the first table that this time have been pushed out by even bigger successes. Our special sympathies go to Showaddywaddy, whose 'You Got What It Takes' just missed at 1001. The only encouragement we can offer is the examples of 'Albatross', 'Bohemian Rhapsody' and 'Honey', which have had re-issues that reached the top two, and 'Crazy For You', which had a re-mix that peaked at two. A sudden new burst of enthusiasm for 'You Got What It Takes' could yet land it back in the Top 1000 five years from now.

Paul Gambaccini ● Jonathan Rice ● Tim Rice

PART ONE

THE UK TOP 1000 SINGLES

IN RANKED ORDER FROM 1955-1993

1 Bryan Adams gets the winner's bouquet for his 16 weeks at number one with '(Everything I Do) I Do It For You'.

THE UK TOP 1000 SINGLES		Weeks				
Rank	Title and Artist	Year	No.1	No.2	No.3	No.4	No.5

Rank	Title and Artist	Year	No.1	No.2	No.3	No.4	No.5
1	**(Everything I Do) I Do It For You** Bryan Adams	1991	16	1	0	2	0
2	**Bohemian Rhapsody/These Are The Days Of Our Lives** Queen	1975	14	1	1	1	0
3	**I Will Always Love You** Whitney Houston	1992	10	2	0	2	0
4	**You're The One That I Want** John Travolta and Olivia Newton-John	1978	9	3	0	0	1
5	**Mull Of Kintyre/Girls' School** Wings	1977	9	1	0	0	2
6	**Diana** Paul Anka	1957	9	0	1	2	0
7	**Two Tribes** Frankie Goes To Hollywood	1984	9	0	1	0	1
8	**Magic Moments** Perry Como	1958	8	2	1	1	0
9	**Stay** Shakespears Sister	1992	8	2	0	0	1
10	**Wonderful Land** Shadows	1962	8	1	1	0	0
11	**It's Now Or Never** Elvis Presley	1960	8	1	0	1	0
12	**Sugar Sugar** Archies	1969	8	0	3	0	0
13	**Young Love** Tab Hunter	1957	7	3	2	0	0
14	**All I Have To Do Is Dream/Claudette** Everly Brothers	1958	7	3	1	1	2
15	**I Remember You** Frank Ifield	1962	7	3	0	1	0
16	**Just Walkin' In The Rain** Johnnie Ray	1956	7	2	1	0	2
17	**Green Green Grass Of Home** Tom Jones	1966	7	1	1	1	1
18	**From Me To You** Beatles	1963	7	1	1	1	0
19	**All Shook Up** Elvis Presley	1957	7	1	1	0	1
20	**Cathy's Clown** Everly Brothers	1960	7	0	1	1	0
21	**Summer Nights** John Travolta and Olivia Newton-John	1978	7	0	1	0	0
22	**Mary's Boy Child** Harry Belafonte	1957	7	0	1	0	0
23	**In The Summertime** Mungo Jerry	1970	7	0	0	1	0
24	**Hello Goodbye** Beatles	1967	7	0	0	0	0
25	**She Loves You** Beatles	1963	6	6	6	0	2
26	**Whatever Will Be Will Be** Doris Day	1956	6	4	1	1	1
27	**Living Doll** Cliff Richard and the Drifters	1959	6	3	2	1	1
28	**What Do You Want To Make Those Eyes At Me For** Emile Ford and the Checkmates	1959	6	3	2	1	0
29	**The Young Ones** Cliff Richard and the Shadows	1962	6	3	0	1	0
30	**Rhythm Is A Dancer** Snap	1992	6	2	2	1	0
31	**Who's Sorry Now** Connie Francis	1958	6	2	1	1	0
32	**I Just Called To Say I Love You** Stevie Wonder	1984	6	2	1	1	0
33	**Two Little Boys** Rolf Harris	1969	6	2	1	0	1
34	**Ride On Time** Black Box	1989	6	2	1	0	1
35	**Carolina Moon/Stupid Cupid** Connie Francis	1958	6	2	0	2	0
36	**Release Me** Engelbert Humperdinck	1967	6	2	0	1	1
37	**Save Your Kisses For Me** Brotherhood Of Man	1976	6	2	0	1	0

Continued

Above **2** 'Bohemian Rhapsody' by Queen is the only single to have been number one in four calendar years (1975, 1976, 1991 and 1992).

Above **4 and 21** John Travolta and Olivia Newton-John averaged eight weeks for their first two singles, but 'The Grease Megamix' which was released for Christmas 1990 fell short of the summit. Left **3** Whitney Houston holds the record for most consecutive number ones in the United States, seven.

THE UK TOP 1000 SINGLES

Rank	Title and Artist	Year	Weeks				
			No.1	No.2	No.3	No.4	No.5

Rank	Title and Artist	Year	No.1	No.2	No.3	No.4	No.5
38	**Those Were The Days** Mary Hopkin	1968	6	2	0	0	1
39	**I Hear You Knocking** Dave Edmunds	1970	6	2	0	0	0
40	**The Wonder Of You** Elvis Presley	1970	6	1	1	1	1
41	**Don't Go Breaking My Heart** Elton John and Kiki Dee	1976	6	1	1	1	0
42	**Wooden Heart** Elvis Presley	1961	6	1	0	1	1
43	**Get Back** Beatles with Billy Preston	1969	6	1	0	0	1
44	**Bye Bye Love** Bay City Rollers	1975	6	1	0	0	1
45	**Hot Love** T. Rex	1971	6	1	0	0	0
46	**Dancing Queen** Abba	1976	6	1	0	0	0
47	**Band Of Gold** Freda Payne	1970	6	0	1	1	0
48	**Karma Chameleon** Culture Club	1983	6	0	1	1	0
49	**Bright Eyes** Art Garfunkel	1979	6	0	1	0	0
50	**No Other Love** Ronnie Hilton	1956	6	0	0	3	1
51	**A Whiter Shade Of Pale** Procol Harum	1967	6	0	0	2	0
52	**Hello** Lionel Richie	1984	6	0	0	1	1
53	**Relax!** Frankie Goes To Hollywood	1983	5	4	5	0	1
54	**Rock Around The Clock** Bill Haley and his Comets	1955	5	4	1	1	1
55	**Rivers Of Babylon** Boney M	1978	5	3	3	1	2
56	**I'll Be Home** Pat Boone	1956	5	3	1	2	0
57	**A Fool Such As I/I Need Your Love Tonight** Elvis Presley	1959	5	3	0	2	2
58	**Without You** Nilsson	1972	5	2	2	0	1
59	**Tears** Ken Dodd	1965	5	2	1	1	3
60	**Maggie May** Rod Stewart	1971	5	2	1	1	0
61	**It's Only Make Believe** Conway Twitty	1958	5	2	1	0	1
62	**Apache** Shadows	1960	5	2	1	0	1
63	**Knock Three Times** Dawn	1971	5	2	1	0	0
64	**Chirpy Chirpy Cheep Cheep** Middle Of The Road	1971	5	2	1	0	0
65	**The Shoop Shoop Song (It's In His Kiss)** Cher	1991	5	2	1	0	0
66	**No Limit** 2 Unlimited	1993	5	2	0	2	1
67	**The Power Of Love** Jennifer Rush	1985	5	2	0	1	1
68	**Day Tripper/We Can Work It Out** Beatles	1965	5	2	0	1	0
69	**Knowing Me Knowing You** Abba	1977	5	2	0	0	0
70	**When** Kalin Twins	1958	5	1	4	0	0
71	**The Last Waltz** Engelbert Humperdinck	1967	5	1	3	2	2
72	**Lovesick Blues** Frank Ifield	1962	5	1	2	1	3
73	**Good Luck Charm** Elvis Presley	1962	5	1	2	1	0
74	**Do They Know It's Christmas** Band Aid	1984	5	1	2	0	1
75	**Travellin' Light** Cliff Richard and the Shadows	1959	5	1	2	0	1
76	**Amazing Grace** Pipes and Drums and Military Band of the Royal Scots Dragoon Guards	1972	5	1	2	0	0
77	**Honky Tonk Women** Rolling Stones	1969	5	1	2	0	0

Continued

Above **5** 'Mull of Kintyre'/'Girls' School' was always listed as a double A-side not because of any consumer interest in the second song, a rocker, but because Paul McCartney had been unsure the first tune, a ballad, would be commercial. He underestimated its appeal by more than two million copies. Left **6** Paul Anka was 16 when he spent nine weeks at number one with 'Diana'. He is seen here in December 1957 playing the piano in London.

Below **7** 'Relax' by Frankie Goes to Hollywood took two chart months to climb to number one, but the follow-up, 'Two Tribes', entered at the top.

Above **10** The Shadows (left to right: Bruce Welch, Hank Marvin, Jet Harris and Tony Meehan) are pictured in 1960, the year of the first of their five number ones without Cliff Richard. Left **9** 'Stay' by Shakespears Sister is the only record by a female duo or group in the all-time top 50. Below Left **8** 'Magic Moments' by Perry Como, the first Bacharach-David song to reach number one, was half of one of the most successful two-sided hits in history, the flip being 'Catch A Falling Star'.

THE UK TOP 1000 SINGLES

Rank	Title and Artist	Year	Weeks				
			No.1	No.2	No.3	No.4	No.5

Rank	Title and Artist	Year	No.1	No.2	No.3	No.4	No.5
78	**Distant Drums** Jim Reeves	1966	5	1	1	1	0
79	**Never Gonna Give You Up** Rick Astley	1987	5	1	1	1	1
80	**Swing The Mood** Jive Bunny and the Mastermixers	1989	5	1	1	1	0
81	**Please Don't Go/Game Boy** KWS	1992	5	1	1	0	1
82	**Blockbuster** Sweet	1973	5	1	1	0	1
83	**My Sweet Lord** George Harrison	1971	5	1	1	0	0
84	**I Want To Hold Your Hand** Beatles	1963	5	1	1	0	0
85	**I Should Be So Lucky** Kylie Minogue	1988	5	1	1	0	0
86	**Long Haired Lover From Liverpool** Little Jimmy Osmond	1972	5	1	0	1	1
87	**Sacrifice/Healing Hands** Elton John	1990	5	1	0	1	1
88	**Way Down** Elvis Presley	1977	5	1	0	1	0
89	**These Are The Days Of Our Lives** Queen	1991	5	1	0	1	0
90	**The One And Only** Chesney Hawkes	1991	5	1	0	0	2
91	**Three Times A Lady** Commodores	1978	5	1	0	0	2
92	**Don't You Want Me** Human League	1981	5	1	0	0	1
93	**Another Brick In The Wall (Part 2)** Pink Floyd	1979	5	1	0	0	1
94	**I Feel Fine** Beatles	1964	5	1	0	0	0
95	**Telstar** Tornados	1962	5	0	2	2	0
96	**Puppy Love** Donny Osmond	1972	5	0	1	2	0
97	**19** Paul Hardcastle	1985	5	0	1	1	0
98	**The Only Way Is Up** Yazz and the Plastic Population	1988	5	0	1	0	0
99	**Uptown Girl** Billy Joel	1983	5	0	1	0	0
100	**Merry Xmas Everybody** Slade	1973	5	0	1	0	0
101	**Cumberland Gap** Lonnie Donegan	1957	5	0	0	1	1
102	**Love Grows (Where My Rosemary Goes)** Edison Lighthouse	1970	5	0	0	1	1
103	**Abba-Esque EP** Erasure	1992	5	0	0	1	0
104	**China In Your Hand** T'Pau	1987	5	0	0	0	2
105	**Stand And Deliver** Adam and the Ants	1981	5	0	0	0	1
106	**Only You** Flying Pickets	1983	5	0	0	0	0
107	**Dream Lover** Bobby Darin	1959	4	4	2	0	2
108	**A Woman In Love** Frankie Laine	1956	4	4	2	0	0
109	**Sailing** Rod Stewart	1975	4	3	2	1	0
110	**I Love You Love Me Love** Gary Glitter	1973	4	3	1	0	0
111	**Fernando** Abba	1976	4	3	0	3	0
112	**Johnny Remember Me** John Leyton	1961	4	3	0	1	1
113	**Only Sixteen** Craig Douglas	1959	4	3	0	1	0
114	**Why** Anthony Newley	1960	4	3	0	1	0
115	**My Ding-A-Ling** Chuck Berry	1972	4	3	0	0	0
116	**We Don't Talk Anymore** Cliff Richard	1979	4	3	0	0	0
117	**As I Love You** Shirley Bassey	1958	4	2	2	1	0

Continued

Rank	Title and Artist	Year	No.1	No.2	No.3	No.4	No.5
118	Ernie (The Fastest Milkman In The West) Benny Hill	1971	4	2	2	0	0
119	Mississippi Pussycat	1976	4	2	1	1	1
120	Lay Down Your Arms Anne Shelton	1956	4	2	1	1	1
121	Ice Ice Baby Vanilla Ice	1990	4	2	1	0	1
122	Unchained Melody Righteous Brothers	1965	4	2	1	0	1
123	Garden Of Eden Frankie Vaughan	1957	4	2	1	0	1
124	Young Girl Union Gap featuring Gary Puckett	1968	4	2	1	0	0
125	I Know Him So Well Elaine Paige and Barbara Dickson	1985	4	2	1	0	0
126	Come On Eileen Dexys Midnight Runners	1982	4	2	1	0	0
127	Lily The Pink Scaffold	1968	4	2	0	3	0
128	I Don't Want To Talk About It/First Cut Is The Deepest Rod Stewart	1977	4	2	0	1	1
129	Eye Of The Tiger Survivor	1982	4	2	0	1	0
130	Massachusetts Bee Gees	1967	4	2	0	1	0
131	You'll Never Walk Alone Gerry and the Pacemakers	1963	4	2	0	1	0
132	Frankie Sister Sledge	1985	4	2	0	1	0
133	Sixteen Tons Tennessee Ernie Ford	1956	4	2	0	0	1
134	Reet Petite Jackie Wilson	1986	4	2	0	0	0
135	I Like It Gerry and the Pacemakers	1963	4	2	0	0	0
136	Eye Level Simon Park Orchestra	1972	4	2	0	0	0
137	Are 'Friends' Electric Tubeway Army	1979	4	2	0	0	0
138	Where Do You Go To My Lovely Peter Sarstedt	1969	4	2	0	0	0
139	I Don't Like Mondays Boomtown Rats	1979	4	2	0	0	0
140	Side Saddle Russ Conway	1959	4	1	3	3	1
141	San Francisco (Be Sure To Wear Some Flowers In Your Hair) Scott McKenzie	1967	4	1	3	0	1
142	Rock-A-Hula Baby/Can't Help Falling In Love Elvis Presley	1962	4	1	2	3	0
143	Tie A Yellow Ribbon Round The Old Oak Tree Dawn	1973	4	1	2	1	0
144	Take My Breath Away Berlin	1986	4	1	2	0	1
145	Nothing's Gonna Stop Us Now Starship	1987	4	1	2	0	1
146	The Good The Bad And The Ugly Hugo Montenegro	1968	4	1	2	0	0
147	Don't Give Up On Us David Soul	1976	4	1	2	0	0
148	What A Wonderful World/Cabaret Louis Armstrong	1968	4	1	1	1	2
149	I'm A Believer Monkees	1967	4	1	1	1	1
150	Mouldy Old Dough Lieutenant Pigeon	1972	4	1	1	1	1
151	Nothing Compares 2 U Sinead O'Connor	1990	4	1	1	1	0
152	Don't Leave Me This Way Communards featuring Sarah Jane Morris	1986	4	1	1	0	1

Continued

11 The artist with the most entries in the Top 1000, Elvis Presley waves to fans while his manager Colonel Tom Parker keeps close watch behind.

THE UK TOP 1000 SINGLES

Rank	Title and Artist	Year	Weeks				
			No.1	No.2	No.3	No.4	No.5

Rank	Title and Artist	Year	No.1	No.2	No.3	No.4	No.5
153	**Dub Be Good To Me** Beats International featuring Lindy Layton	1990	4	1	1	0	1
154	**Ebeneezer Goode** Shamen	1992	4	1	1	0	0
155	**I'm The Leader Of The Gang (I Am)** Gary Glitter	1973	4	1	1	0	0
156	**Goodnight Girl** Wet Wet Wet	1992	4	1	1	0	0
157	**Are You Lonesome Tonight** Elvis Presley	1961	4	1	1	0	0
158	**I'm Still Waiting** Diana Ross	1971	4	1	1	0	0
159	**Easy Lover** Philip Bailey (duet with Phil Collins)	1985	4	1	1	0	0
160	**Killer** Adamski	1990	4	1	0	2	0
161	**I'd Like To Teach The World To Sing** New Seekers	1971	4	1	0	2	0
162	**Into The Groove** Madonna	1985	4	1	0	2	0
163	**Show Me Heaven** Maria McKee	1990	4	1	0	2	0
164	**Little Sister/His Latest Flame** Elvis Presley	1961	4	1	0	1	1
165	**Metal Guru** T. Rex	1972	4	1	0	1	0
166	**Always On My Mind** Pet Shop Boys	1987	4	1	0	1	0
167	**Prince Charming** Adam and the Ants	1981	4	1	0	1	0
168	**When The Going Gets Tough, The Tough Get Going** Billy Ocean	1986	4	1	0	0	1
169	**Eternal Flame** Bangles	1989	4	1	0	0	1
170	**Young At Heart** Bluebells	1993	4	1	0	0	1
171	**My Old Man's A Dustman** Lonnie Donegan	1960	4	1	0	0	1
172	**She** Charles Aznavour	1974	4	1	0	0	1
173	**Heart Of Glass** Blondie	1979	4	1	0	0	0
174	**Surrender** Elvis Presley	1961	4	1	0	0	0
175	**Tiger Feet** Mud	1974	4	1	0	0	0
176	**Sugar Baby Love** Rubettes	1974	4	1	0	0	0
177	**Mary's Boy Child-Oh My Lord** Boney M	1978	4	1	0	0	0
178	**Every Breath You Take** Police	1983	4	1	0	0	0
179	**The Sun Ain't Gonna Shine Anymore** Walker Brothers	1966	4	1	0	0	0
180	**Cum On Feel The Noize** Slade	1973	4	1	0	0	0
181	**True** Spandau Ballet	1983	4	1	0	0	0
182	**Coz I Luv You** Slade	1971	4	0	3	0	0
183	**Memories Are Made Of This** Dean Martin	1956	4	0	2	1	1
184	**Save Your Love** Renee and Renato	1982	4	0	2	0	1
185	**I Feel Love** Donna Summer	1977	4	0	2	0	1
186	**Back To Life (However Do You Want Me)** Soul II Soul featuring Caron Wheeler	1989	4	0	2	0	0
187	**Seasons In The Sun** Terry Jacks	1974	4	0	2	0	0
188	**Get It On** T. Rex	1971	4	0	1	2	0
189	**I Will Survive** Gloria Gaynor	1979	4	0	1	1	1
190	**The Reflex** Duran Duran	1984	4	0	1	1	1
191	**See My Baby Jive** Wizzard	1973	4	0	1	1	0

Continued

12 The Archies (Archie, Betty and Veronica are shown) meet American television comedian Soupy Sales in 1965, not realising they will have an international number one in 1969 and that 20 years later his sons, Hunt and Tony Sales, will join David Bowie and Reeves Gabrels to form Tin Machine.

13 Arthur Kelm found fame as film star Tab Hunter.

Rank	Title and Artist	Year	Weeks No.1	No.2	No.3	No.4	No.5
192	You're My World Cilla Black	1964	4	0	1	1	0
193	Turtle Power Partners In Kryme	1990	4	0	1	1	0
194	Yellow Submarine/Eleanor Rigby Beatles	1966	4	0	1	0	1
195	Wuthering Heights Kate Bush	1978	4	0	1	0	1
196	With A Little Help From My Friends/She's Leaving Home Wet Wet Wet/Billy Bragg with Cara Tivey	1988	4	0	1	0	1
197	You Win Again Bee Gees	1987	4	0	1	0	0
198	Nothing's Gonna Change My Love For You Glenn Medeiros	1988	4	0	1	0	0
199	Dancing In The Street David Bowie and Mick Jagger	1985	4	0	1	0	0
200	Something's Gotten Hold Of My Heart Marc Almond featuring Gene Pitney	1989	4	0	1	0	0
201	Don't Stand So Close To Me Police	1980	4	0	1	0	0
202	Vogue Madonna	1990	4	0	0	2	0
203	The Name Of The Game Abba	1977	4	0	0	1	1
204	Imagine John Lennon	1981	4	0	0	1	0
205	Lonely This Christmas Mud	1974	4	0	0	1	0
206	Green Door Shakin' Stevens	1981	4	0	0	1	0
207	These Boots Are Made For Walking Nancy Sinatra	1966	4	0	0	1	0
208	Mistletoe And Wine Cliff Richard	1988	4	0	0	0	1
209	It's My Party Dave Stewart and Barbara Gaskin	1981	4	0	0	0	0
210	Young Love Donny Osmond	1973	4	0	0	0	0
211	It Doesn't Matter Anymore Buddy Holly	1959	3	5	3	0	0
212	Hoots Mon Lord Rockingham's XI	1958	3	5	2	0	1
213	Runaway Del Shannon	1961	3	5	1	0	1
214	The Next Time/Bachelor Boy Cliff Richard	1962	3	5	0	1	1
215	Singing The Blues Guy Mitchell	1956	3	4	2	3	1
216	Poor People Of Paris Winifred Atwell	1956	3	4	2	0	1
217	Please Don't Tease Cliff Richard and the Shadows	1960	3	4	1	2	0
218	Under The Moon Of Love Showaddywaddy	1976	3	4	1	1	0
219	Why Do Fools Fall In Love Teenagers featuring Frankie Lymon	1956	3	4	1	0	1
220	Especially For You Kylie Minogue and Jason Donovan	1988	3	4	1	0	0
221	Y.M.C.A. Village People	1978	3	4	0	1	0
222	What Do You Want Adam Faith	1959	3	4	0	1	0
223	It's Almost Tomorrow Dreamweavers	1956	3	3	6	0	0
224	You Don't Know Helen Shapiro	1961	3	3	3	1	0
225	Walkin' Back To Happiness Helen Shapiro	1961	3	3	1	2	0
226	End Of The Road Boyz II Men	1992	3	3	1	1	0

Continued

Rank	Title and Artist	Year	No.1	No.2	No.3	No.4	No.5
227	**Whole Lotta Woman** Marvin Rainwater	1958	3	3	1	0	1
228	**Careless Whisper** George Michael	1984	3	3	1	0	1
229	**Return To Sender** Elvis Presley	1962	3	3	1	0	0
230	**All You Need Is Love** Beatles	1967	3	3	1	0	0
231	**Oh Pretty Woman** Roy Orbison	1964	3	3	0	2	0
232	**How Do You Do It** Gerry and the Pacemakers	1963	3	3	0	1	0
233	**Whispering Grass** Windsor Davies and Don Estelle	1975	3	3	0	1	0
234	**Good Timin'** Jimmy Jones	1960	3	3	0	0	1
235	**Take A Chance On Me** Abba	1978	3	3	0	0	0
236	**Bridge Over Troubled Water** Simon and Garfunkel	1970	3	2	2	2	0
237	**Hey Girl Don't Bother Me** Tams	1971	3	2	2	0	0
238	**Back Home** England World Cup Squad	1970	3	2	2	0	0
239	**The Carnival Is Over** Seekers	1965	3	2	1	3	0
240	**If You Leave Me Now** Chicago	1976	3	2	1	2	0
241	**Fame** Irene Cara	1982	3	2	1	1	0
242	**When You're In Love With A Beautiful Woman** Dr. Hook	1979	3	2	1	1	0
243	**I Heard It Through The Grapevine** Marvin Gaye	1969	3	2	1	0	1
244	**A Hard Day's Night** Beatles	1964	3	2	1	0	1
245	**Strangers In The Night** Frank Sinatra	1966	3	2	1	0	1
246	**Gonna Make You A Star** David Essex	1974	3	2	1	0	1
247	**This Ole House** Shakin' Stevens	1981	3	2	1	0	0
248	**Papa Don't Preach** Madonna	1986	3	2	1	0	0
249	**Red Red Wine** UB40	1983	3	2	1	0	0
250	**Bad Moon Rising** Creedence Clearwater Revival	1969	3	2	1	0	0
251	**The Lady In Red** Chris De Burgh	1986	3	2	1	0	0
252	**Wherever I Lay My Hat (That's My Home)** Paul Young	1983	3	2	1	0	0
253	**Grandad** Clive Dunn	1970	3	2	0	1	0
254	**Wand'rin' Star** Lee Marvin	1970	3	2	0	1	0
255	**Mony Mony** Tommy James and the Shondells	1968	3	2	0	1	0
256	**Cinderella Rockefella** Esther and Abi Ofarim	1968	3	2	0	1	0
257	**Chain Reaction** Diana Ross	1986	3	2	0	1	0
258	**I Wanna Sex You Up** Color Me Badd	1991	3	2	0	1	0
259	**Help!** Beatles	1965	3	2	0	0	2
260	**I Want To Wake Up With You** Boris Gardiner	1986	3	2	0	0	2
261	**Ghost Town** Specials	1981	3	2	0	0	1
262	**I Feel For You** Chaka Khan	1984	3	2	0	0	1
263	**Tower Of Strength** Frankie Vaughan	1961	3	2	0	0	1
264	**The Lion Sleeps Tonight** Tight Fit	1982	3	2	0	0	0

Continued

Above **14 and 20** The Everly Brothers had four number ones in the UK and US, but only 'All I Have To Do Is Dream' and 'Cathy's Clown' topped both charts. Left **15** Frank Ifield was in the charts with 'The Wayward Wind' in March, 1963, when he strayed into the audience of *Thank Your Lucky Stars* to sign autographs.

Rank	Title and Artist	Year	Weeks No.1	No.2	No.3	No.4	No.5
265	**Summer Holiday** Cliff Richard and the Shadows	1963	3	2	0	0	0
266	**Down Under** Men At Work	1983	3	2	0	0	0
267	**Hold Me Close** David Essex	1975	3	2	0	0	0
268	**Billy Don't Be A Hero** Paper Lace	1974	3	2	0	0	0
269	**When A Child Is Born (Soleado)** Johnny Mathis	1976	3	2	0	0	0
270	**99 Red Balloons** Nena	1984	3	2	0	0	0
271	**Jailhouse Rock** Elvis Presley	1958	3	1	4	1	0
272	**Yes Tonight Josephine** Johnnie Ray	1957	3	1	3	0	0
273	**Do The Bartman** Simpsons	1991	3	1	3	0	0
274	**Walk Right Back/Ebony Eyes** Everly Brothers	1961	3	1	2	3	0
275	**Puppet On A String** Sandie Shaw	1967	3	1	2	1	1
276	**Matchstalk Men And Matchstalk Cats And Dogs** Brian and Michael	1978	3	1	2	1	0
277	**Silver Lady** David Soul	1977	3	1	2	1	0
278	**That'll Be The Day** Crickets	1957	3	1	2	0	1
279	**I Love To Love (But My Baby Loves To Dance)** Tina Charles	1976	3	1	2	0	1
280	**I Can't Give You Anything (But My Love)** Stylistics	1975	3	1	2	0	0
281	**It's All In The Game** Tommy Edwards	1958	3	1	1	2	1
282	**Deeply Dippy** Right Said Fred	1992	3	1	1	2	1
283	**So You Win Again** Hot Chocolate	1977	3	1	1	1	1
284	**Rock Your Baby** George McCrae	1974	3	1	1	1	0
285	**Tell Laura I Love Her** Ricky Valance	1960	3	1	1	1	0
286	**One Night/I Got Stung** Elvis Presley	1959	3	1	1	1	0
287	**Reach Out I'll Be There** Four Tops	1966	3	1	1	1	0
288	**Do You Really Want To Hurt Me** Culture Club	1982	3	1	1	1	0
289	**Freedom** Wham!	1984	3	1	1	1	0
290	**Anyone Who Had A Heart** Cilla Black	1964	3	1	1	1	0
291	**Son Of My Father** Chicory Tip	1972	3	1	1	1	0
292	**Do You Love Me** Brian Poole and the Tremeloes	1963	3	1	1	0	1
293	**Ain't No Doubt** Jimmy Nail	1992	3	1	1	0	1
294	**When I Need You** Leo Sayer	1977	3	1	1	0	1
295	**Stand By Your Man** Tammy Wynette	1975	3	1	1	0	1
296	**I Think We're Alone Now** Tiffany	1988	3	1	1	0	1
297	**Everything I Own** Ken Boothe	1974	3	1	1	0	1
298	**Woman In Love** Barbra Streisand	1980	3	1	1	0	0
299	**Baby Jane** Rod Stewart	1983	3	1	1	0	0
300	**School's Out** Alice Cooper	1972	3	1	1	0	0
301	**Ticket To Ride** Beatles	1965	3	1	1	0	0
302	**Mama Weer All Crazee Now** Slade	1972	3	1	1	0	0

Continued

Left **16** Johnnie Ray, the only pop star ever to not attempt to conceal his hearing aid, emotes during a photo call at the Dorchester Hotel in London.

Below **17** Tom Jones rehearses for a 1966 Christmas television show.

THE UK TOP 1000 SINGLES

			Weeks				
Rank	Title and Artist	Year	No.1	No.2	No.3	No.4	No.5

Rank	Title and Artist	Year	No.1	No.2	No.3	No.4	No.5
303	**Daydreamer/The Puppy Song** David Cassidy	1973	3	1	1	0	0
304	**Like A Prayer** Madonna	1989	3	1	1	0	0
305	**Ebony And Ivory** Paul McCartney with Stevie Wonder	1982	3	1	1	0	0
306	**Silence Is Golden** Tremeloes	1967	3	1	0	3	0
307	**I'm Alive** Hollies	1965	3	1	0	2	0
308	**Crying** Don McLean	1980	3	1	0	2	0
309	**Kung Fu Fighting** Carl Douglas	1974	3	1	0	2	0
310	**Living Doll** Cliff Richard and the Young Ones	1986	3	1	0	2	0
311	**Super Trouper** Abba	1980	3	1	0	1	2
312	**Making Your Mind Up** Bucks Fizz	1981	3	1	0	1	1
313	**It's A Sin** Pet Shop Boys	1987	3	1	0	1	1
314	**Give It Up** KC and the Sunshine Band	1983	3	1	0	1	1
315	**A Different Corner** George Michael	1986	3	1	0	1	0
316	**Theme From M★A★S★H (Suicide Is Painless)** Mash	1980	3	1	0	1	0
317	**Five Live EP** George Michael and Queen	1993	3	1	0	1	0
318	**Can't Buy Me Love** Beatles	1964	3	1	0	1	0
319	**Wayward Wind** Frank Ifield	1963	3	1	0	1	0
320	**Sunday Girl** Blondie	1979	3	1	0	1	0
321	**Give A Little Love** Bay City Rollers	1975	3	1	0	1	0
322	**Every Loser Wins** Nick Berry	1986	3	1	0	1	0
323	**I Don't Wanna Dance** Eddy Grant	1982	3	1	0	1	0
324	**Seven Tears** Goombay Dance Band	1982	3	1	0	1	0
325	**Christmas Alphabet** Dickie Valentine	1955	3	1	0	1	0
326	**Woodstock** Matthews Southern Comfort	1970	3	1	0	1	0
327	**Pretty Flamingo** Manfred Mann	1966	3	1	0	1	0
328	**Love Me For A Reason** Osmonds	1974	3	1	0	0	2
329	**You To Me Are Everything** Real Thing	1976	3	1	0	0	1
330	**One Day At A Time** Lena Martell	1979	3	1	0	0	1
331	**She's Not You** Elvis Presley	1962	3	1	0	0	1
332	**Let's Dance** David Bowie	1983	3	1	0	0	1
333	**Pass The Dutchie** Musical Youth	1982	3	1	0	0	1
334	**The Last Time** Rolling Stones	1965	3	1	0	0	0
335	**Stand By Me** Ben E. King	1961	3	1	0	0	0
336	**Heart** Pet Shop Boys	1988	3	1	0	0	0
337	**(There's) Always Something There To Remind Me** Sandie Shaw	1964	3	1	0	0	0
338	**Message In A Bottle** Police	1979	3	1	0	0	0
339	**January** Pilot	1975	3	1	0	0	0
340	**Bad To Me** Billy J Kramer and the Dakotas	1963	3	0	3	0	0
341	**Needles And Pins** Searchers	1964	3	0	2	1	0
342	**Ballad Of John And Yoko** Beatles	1969	3	0	2	1	0
343	**Chanson D'Amour** Manhattan Transfer	1977	3	0	2	0	1
344	**In The Year 2525 (Exordium And Terminus)** Zager and Evans	1969	3	0	2	0	1

Continued

Above **18, 24, 25 and 43** In a photo taken in 1963, with no attempt at image control, the Beatles are shown smoking and drinking. Left **22** Harry Belafonte, shown during a television performance, never had another number one, but his song went back to the top in a 1978 version by Boney M.

Left **23** Mungo Jerry were driven to the top by lead vocalist and songwriter Ray Dorset (standing).

Below **26** Not only did Doris Day have one of the top hits of the rock era, she had the longest-running female number one of the pre-rock years, the nine-week wonder 'Secret Love'.

Rank	Title and Artist	Year	No.1	No.2	No.3	No.4	No.5
345	Baby Come Back Equals	1968	3	0	2	0	0
346	Itsy Bitsy Teeny Weeny Yellow Polka Dot Bikini Bombalurina	1990	3	0	2	0	0
347	Shaddap You Face Joe Dolce Music Theatre	1981	3	0	2	0	0
348	Diamonds Jet Harris and Tony Meehan	1963	3	0	1	2	0
349	I Want To Know What Love Is Foreigner	1984	3	0	1	1	1
350	Spirit In The Sky Doctor and the Medics	1986	3	0	1	1	1
351	Ob-La-Di Ob-La-Da Marmalade	1968	3	0	1	1	0
352	That's What I Like Jive Bunny and the Mastermixers	1989	3	0	1	1	0
353	Get Off Of My Cloud Rolling Stones	1965	3	0	1	1	0
354	You Got It (The Right Stuff) New Kids On The Block	1989	3	0	1	1	0
355	Something In The Air Thunderclap Newman	1969	3	0	1	0	1
356	Going Underground/Dreams Of Children Jam	1980	3	0	1	0	0
357	Long Live Love Sandie Shaw	1965	3	0	1	0	0
358	The Chicken Song Spitting Image	1986	3	0	1	0	0
359	A Town Called Malice Jam	1982	3	0	1	0	0
360	Ferry 'Cross The Mersey Christians, Holly Johnson, Gerry Marsden and Stock Aitken Waterman	1989	3	0	1	0	0
361	Let It Be Ferry Aid	1987	3	0	1	0	0
362	Skweeze Me Pleeze Me Slade	1973	3	0	0	1	0
363	Do They Know It's Christmas Band Aid II	1989	3	0	0	1	0
364	First Time Robin Beck	1988	3	0	0	0	2
365	Orinoco Flow Enya	1988	3	0	0	0	2
366	Michelle Overlanders	1966	3	0	0	0	1
367	The Story Of My Life Michael Holliday	1958	2	6	1	0	0
368	Gamblin' Man/Putting On The Style Lonnie Donegan	1957	2	5	0	2	0
369	Mack The Knife Bobby Darin	1959	2	4	2	0	1
370	Confessin' Frank Ifield	1963	2	4	1	1	0
371	Night Fever Bee Gees	1978	2	4	1	0	0
372	Somethin' Stupid Nancy Sinatra and Frank Sinatra	1967	2	4	0	0	1
373	Saving All My Love For You Whitney Houston	1985	2	4	0	0	0
374	Hey Jude Beatles	1968	2	3	1	1	0
375	Butterfly Andy Williams	1957	2	3	1	1	0
376	Oh Carolina Shaggy	1993	2	3	1	0	1
377	Any Dream Will Do Jason Donovan	1991	2	3	1	0	0
378	Glad All Over Dave Clark Five	1963	2	3	0	2	0
379	I Love You Cliff Richard and the Shadows	1960	2	3	0	2	0
380	It's Over Roy Orbison	1964	2	3	0	1	2

Continued

Above **27 and 29** 'The Young Ones' by Cliff Richard and the Shadows (formerly Cliff Richard and the Drifters) was the first single by a British act to enter the chart at number one.

Left **28** The Emile Ford and the Checkmates title 'What Do You Want To Make Those Eyes At Me For?' is the longest number one question.

Rank	Title and Artist	Year	Weeks No.1	No.2	No.3	No.4	No.5
381	**Spirit In The Sky** Norman Greenbaum	1970	2	3	0	1	1
382	**I Wanna Dance With Somebody (Who Loves Me)** Whitney Houston	1987	2	3	0	1	0
383	**Crying In The Chapel** Elvis Presley	1965	2	3	0	0	1
384	**Goody Two Shoes** Adam Ant	1982	2	3	0	0	1
385	**Too Many Broken Hearts** Jason Donovan	1989	2	3	0	0	0
386	**Tainted Love** Soft Cell	1982	2	3	0	0	0
387	**Would I Lie To You** Charles and Eddie	1992	2	2	4	1	0
388	**Only The Lonely** Roy Orbison	1960	2	2	2	2	1
389	**I Can't Stop Loving You** Ray Charles	1962	2	2	2	1	0
390	**Three Steps To Heaven** Eddie Cochran	1960	2	2	2	0	1
391	**Have I The Right** Honeycombs	1964	2	2	2	0	0
392	**On The Street Where You Live** Vic Damone	1958	2	2	1	3	0
393	**He Ain't Heavy He's My Brother** Hollies	1969	2	2	1	2	4
394	**Come Outside** Mike Sarne with Wendy Richard	1962	2	2	1	2	0
395	**When Will I See You Again** Three Degrees	1974	2	2	1	1	0
396	**Little Children** Billy J. Kramer and the Dakotas	1964	2	2	1	1	0
397	**Everlasting Love** Love Affair	1968	2	2	1	1	0
398	**I Only Have Eyes For You** Art Garfunkel	1975	2	2	1	1	0
399	**Moon River** Danny Williams	1961	2	2	1	0	1
400	**Rat Trap** Boomtown Rats	1978	2	2	1	0	1
401	**I'm Into Something Good** Herman's Hermits	1964	2	2	1	0	1
402	**3 AM Eternal** KLF featuring the Children Of The Revolution	1991	2	2	1	0	1
403	**Heaven Is A Place On Earth** Belinda Carlisle	1987	2	2	1	0	1
404	**All Kinds Of Everything** Dana	1970	2	2	1	0	1
405	**One Day In Your Life** Michael Jackson	1981	2	2	1	0	1
406	**You Can't Hurry Love** Phil Collins	1982	2	2	1	0	0
407	**Pump Up The Volume/Anitina (The First Time I See She Dance)** M/A/R/R/S	1987	2	2	1	0	0
408	**The Mighty Quinn** Manfred Mann	1968	2	2	1	0	0
409	**December '63 (Oh What A Night)** Four Seasons	1976	2	2	1	0	0
410	**Total Eclipse Of The Heart** Bonnie Tyler	1985	2	2	1	0	0
411	**Use It Up And Wear It Out** Odyssey	1980	2	2	1	0	0
412	**Combine Harvester (Brand New Key)** Wurzels	1976	2	2	1	0	0
413	**Telegram Sam** T. Rex	1972	2	2	1	0	0
414	**Roulette** Russ Conway	1959	2	2	0	2	1
415	**I Got You Babe** Sonny and Cher	1965	2	2	0	2	0
416	**Baby Now That I've Found You** Foundations	1967	2	2	0	1	1

Continued

THE UK TOP 1000 SINGLES

Rank	Title and Artist	Year	Weeks				
			No.1	No.2	No.3	No.4	No.5

Rank	Title and Artist	Year	No.1	No.2	No.3	No.4	No.5
417	The Land Of Make Believe Bucks Fizz	1981	2	2	0	1	1
418	Space Oddity David Bowie	1969	2	2	0	1	1
419	Do Wah Diddy Diddy Manfred Mann	1968	2	2	0	1	1
420	I'll Never Find Another You Seekers	1965	2	2	0	1	1
421	Wake Me Up Before You Go-Go Wham!	1984	2	2	0	1	1
422	Running Bear Johnny Preston	1960	2	2	0	1	0
423	World In Motion... Englandneworder	1990	2	2	0	1	0
424	I'm Your Man Wham!	1985	2	2	0	1	0
425	If Telly Savalas	1975	2	2	0	1	0
426	Vincent Don McLean	1972	2	2	0	0	2
427	Good Vibrations Beach Boys	1966	2	2	0	0	2
428	The Sun Always Shines On T.V. A-Ha	1985	2	2	0	0	1
429	The Tide Is High Blondie	1980	2	2	0	0	1
430	Groovy Kind Of Love Phil Collins	1988	2	2	0	0	1
431	Geno Dexy's Midnight Runners	1980	2	2	0	0	1
432	The Edge Of Heaven/Where Did Your Heart Go Wham!	1986	2	2	0	0	1
433	I Knew You Were Waiting (For Me) Aretha Franklin and George Michael	1987	2	2	0	0	1
434	Dizzy Vic Reeves and the Wonderstuff	1991	2	2	0	0	0
435	Coward Of The County Kenny Rogers	1980	2	2	0	0	0
436	Devil Gate Drive Suzi Quatro	1974	2	2	0	0	0
437	Waterloo Abba	1974	2	2	0	0	0
438	There's No One Quite Like Grandma St.Winifred's School Choir	1980	2	2	0	0	0
439	Paperback Writer Beatles	1966	2	2	0	0	0
440	(If Paradise Is) Half As Nice Amen Corner	1969	2	2	0	0	0
441	The Final Countdown Europe	1986	2	1	3	1	1
442	Poetry In Motion Johnny Tillotson	1960	2	1	3	0	1
443	Sweets For My Sweet Searchers	1963	2	1	3	0	0
444	Woman John Lennon	1981	2	1	2	1	0
445	La Isla Bonita Madonna	1987	2	1	2	0	1
446	With A Girl Like You Troggs	1966	2	1	2	0	1
447	Mamma Mia Abba	1975	2	1	2	0	1
448	(I Can't Get No) Satisfaction Rolling Stones	1965	2	1	2	0	0
449	All Around The World Lisa Stansfield	1989	2	1	2	0	0
450	You're The First The Last My Everything Barry White	1974	2	1	1	2	1
451	Sleeping Satellite Tasmin Archer	1992	2	1	1	2	0
452	Jumping Jack Flash Rolling Stones	1968	2	1	1	1	1
453	Double Barrel Dave and Ansil Collins	1971	2	1	1	1	1
454	The Power Snap!	1990	2	1	1	1	0
455	Free Deniece Williams	1977	2	1	1	1	0
456	Ashes To Ashes David Bowie	1980	2	1	1	1	0
457	Mr. Tambourine Man Byrds	1965	2	1	1	1	0

Continued

31 and 35 Nineteen–year–old Connie Francis is shown at a 1958 London reception at which she inquired "Where are the songs the younger generation will have to look back on? 'The Purple People Eater' and 'Witch Doctor' are nothing like those wonderful old evergreens such as 'Blue Skies'."

30 The hook line of 'The Power' by Snap! was a sample of a Jocelyn Brown record.

THE UK TOP 1000 SINGLES

Rank	Title and Artist	Year	Weeks				
			No.1	No.2	No.3	No.4	No.5

Rank	Title and Artist	Year	No.1	No.2	No.3	No.4	No.5
458	I'm Not In Love 10 C.C.	1975	2	1	1	1	0
459	Don't Let The Sun Go Down On Me George Michael and Elton John	1991	2	1	1	1	0
460	You'll Never Stop Me Loving You Sonia	1989	2	1	1	1	0
461	How Can I Be Sure David Cassidy	1972	2	1	1	1	0
462	Ring My Bell Anita Ward	1979	2	1	1	1	0
463	Xanadu Olivia Newton-John and the Electric Light Orchestra	1980	2	1	1	1	0
464	Don't Throw Your Love Away Searchers	1964	2	1	1	1	0
465	Sunny Afternoon Kinks	1966	2	1	1	0	2
466	Too Shy Kajagoogoo	1983	2	1	1	0	1
467	Being With You Smokey Robinson	1981	2	1	1	0	1
468	Blue Moon Marcels	1961	2	1	1	0	1
469	Brass In Pocket Pretenders	1979	2	1	1	0	1
470	Clair Gilbert O'Sullivan	1972	2	1	1	0	1
471	Tragedy Bee Gees	1979	2	1	1	0	0
472	Let The Heartaches Begin Long John Baldry	1967	2	1	1	0	0
473	Congratulations Cliff Richard	1968	2	1	1	0	0
474	Oh Boy Mud	1975	2	1	1	0	0
475	Theme From S Express S Express	1988	2	1	1	0	0
476	Atomic Blondie	1980	2	1	1	0	0
477	Jack Your Body Steve 'Silk' Hurley	1987	2	1	1	0	0
478	Make Me Smile (Come Up And See Me) Steve Harley and Cockney Rebel	1975	2	1	1	0	0
479	Somebody Help Me Spencer Davis Group	1966	2	1	1	0	0
480	Star Trekkin' Firm	1987	2	1	1	0	0
481	What's Another Year Johnny Logan	1980	2	1	1	0	0
482	Merry Christmas Everyone Shakin' Stevens	1985	2	1	1	0	0
483	Is There Something I Should Know Duran Duran	1983	2	1	1	0	0
484	A World Without Love Peter and Gordon	1964	2	1	0	2	1
485	A Good Heart Feargal Sharkey	1985	2	1	0	2	0
486	I Owe You Nothing Bros	1988	2	1	0	2	0
487	Baby Jump Mungo Jerry	1971	2	1	0	1	1
488	You Really Got Me Kinks	1964	2	1	0	1	1
489	The Winner Takes It All Abba	1980	2	1	0	1	0
490	Black Or White Michael Jackson	1991	2	1	0	1	0
491	Yeh Yeh Georgie Fame and the Blue Flames	1964	2	1	0	1	0
492	Too Much Too Young (EP) Special AKA featuring Rico	1980	2	1	0	1	0
493	You Spin Me Round (Like A Record) Dead Or Alive	1984	2	1	0	0	1
494	La Bamba Los Lobos	1987	2	1	0	0	1
495	We Are The World USA For Africa	1985	2	1	0	0	1
496	House Of Fun Madness	1982	2	1	0	0	1
497	Sealed With A Kiss Jason Donovan	1989	2	1	0	0	1

Continued

32 Stevie Wonder was asked to provide songs for the film *The Woman In Red* by friend Dionne Warwick, who co-ordinated the music. One proved to be his biggest British success, 'I Just Called To Say I Love You'. Below **33** Rolf Harris performs at the Down Under club.

THE UK TOP 1000 SINGLES

Rank	Title and Artist	Year	Weeks				
			No.1	No.2	No.3	No.4	No.5

Rank	Title and Artist	Year	No.1	No.2	No.3	No.4	No.5
498	Should I Stay Or Should I Go Clash	1982	2	1	0	0	1
499	The Joker Steve Miller Band	1990	2	1	0	0	0
500	Everything I Own Boy George	1987	2	1	0	0	0
501	Belfast Child Simple Minds	1989	2	1	0	0	0
502	Hangin' Tough New Kids On The Block	1990	2	1	0	0	0
503	Pipes Of Peace Paul McCartney	1983	2	1	0	0	0
504	Under Pressure Queen and David Bowie	1981	2	1	0	0	0
505	Beat Surrender Jam	1982	2	1	0	0	0
506	You've Lost That Lovin' Feelin' Righteous Brothers	1965	2	0	3	2	0
507	This Is My Song Petula Clark	1967	2	0	3	1	0
508	Get Down Gilbert O'Sullivan	1973	2	0	3	0	0
509	Temptation Everly Brothers	1961	2	0	2	1	2
510	West End Girls Pet Shop Boys	1985	2	0	2	1	1
511	Working My Way Back To You-Forgive Me Girl Detroit Spinners	1980	2	0	2	0	1
512	Jealous Guy Roxy Music	1981	2	0	2	0	0
513	One Moment In Time Whitney Houston	1988	2	0	2	0	0
514	Feels Like I'm In Love Kelly Marie	1980	2	0	1	1	1
515	You'll Never Walk Alone Crowd	1985	2	0	1	1	0
516	Don't Turn Around Aswad	1988	2	0	1	1	0
517	Baby Love Supremes	1964	2	0	1	0	1
518	I Just Can't Stop Loving You Michael Jackson	1987	2	0	1	0	1
519	Happy Talk Captain Sensible	1982	2	0	1	0	0
520	Lady Madonna Beatles	1968	2	0	0	1	0
521	A Little Peace Nicole	1982	2	0	0	1	0
522	Great Balls Of Fire Jerry Lee Lewis	1957	2	0	0	0	2
523	Bring Your Daughter...To The Slaughter Iron Maiden	1991	2	0	0	0	0
524	Smoke Gets In Your Eyes Platters	1959	1	6	1	1	0
525	Albatross Fleetwood Mac	1968	1	5	1	2	2
526	Welcome Home Peters and Lee	1973	1	5	0	2	1
527	Don't Cry For Me Argentina Julie Covington	1976	1	5	0	0	1
528	Do You Mind Anthony Newley	1960	1	4	0	2	0
529	Tears Of A Clown Smokey Robinson and the Miracles	1970	1	4	0	1	1
530	Angelo Brotherhood Of Man	1977	1	3	1	1	1
531	Sailor Petula Clark	1961	1	3	1	1	0
532	It's Not Unusual Tom Jones	1965	1	3	1	0	0
533	Caravan Of Love Housemartins	1986	1	3	1	0	0
534	It's All Over Now Rolling Stones	1964	1	3	0	2	0
535	Barbados Typically Tropical	1975	1	3	0	1	1
536	Hit Me With Your Rhythm Stick Ian and the Blockheads	1978	1	3	0	1	0

Continued

34 Katrine Quinol of Black Box is shown, but it was samplings of Loleatta Holloway from the 1980 disco hit 'Love Sensation' that provided the vocals on 'Ride On Time'.

THE UK TOP 1000 SINGLES

Rank	Title and Artist	Year	Weeks				
			No.1	No.2	No.3	No.4	No.5

Rank	Title and Artist	Year	No.1	No.2	No.3	No.4	No.5
537	**The Twelfth Of Never** Donny Osmond	1973	1	3	0	1	0
538	**I'll Never Fall In Love Again** Bobbie Gentry	1969	1	3	0	1	0
539	**You Wear It Well** Rod Stewart	1972	1	3	0	1	0
540	**Hand On Your Heart** Kylie Minogue	1989	1	3	0	1	0
541	**Respectable** Mel and Kim	1987	1	3	0	0	1
542	**Keep On Running** Spencer Davis Group	1965	1	3	0	0	0
543	**Forever And Ever** Slik	1976	1	3	0	0	0
544	**Together We Are Beautiful** Fern Kinney	1980	1	3	0	0	0
545	**You Won't Find Another Fool Like Me** New Seekers	1973	1	2	4	1	1
546	**Rock And Roll Waltz** Kay Starr	1956	1	2	3	4	1
547	**Here Comes Summer** Jerry Keller	1959	1	2	2	1	1
548	**Nut Rocker** B. Bumble and the Stingers	1962	1	2	2	1	1
549	**Yellow River** Christie	1970	1	2	2	1	0
550	**Rock-A-Billy** Guy Mitchell	1957	1	2	2	1	0
551	**Yes Sir I Can Boogie** Baccara	1977	1	2	2	1	0
552	**Reach For The Stars/Climb Ev'ry Mountain** Shirley Bassey	1961	1	2	2	0	2
553	**Tears On My Pillow** Johnny Nash	1975	1	2	2	0	1
554	**I Got You Babe** UB40 featuring Chrissie Hynde	1985	1	2	2	0	0
555	**Cars** Gary Numan	1979	1	2	2	0	0
556	**Perfect** Fairground Attraction	1988	1	2	2	0	0
557	**Well I Ask You** Eden Kane	1961	1	2	1	2	3
558	**Lucille** Kenny Rogers	1977	1	2	1	2	1
559	**Je T'Aime...Moi Non Plus** Jane Birkin and Serge Gainsbourg	1969	1	2	1	2	0
560	**Move Closer** Phyllis Nelson	1985	1	2	1	2	0
561	**Rock Me Amadeus** Falco	1986	1	2	1	1	1
562	**I've Gotta Get A Message To You** Bee Gees	1968	1	2	1	1	0
563	**Figaro** Brotherhood Of Man	1978	1	2	1	1	0
564	**You're Driving Me Crazy** Temperance Seven	1961	1	2	1	1	0
565	**Annie's Song** John Denver	1974	1	2	1	0	2
566	**Juliet** Four Pennies	1964	1	2	1	0	2
567	**Rubber Bullets** 10 C.C.	1973	1	2	1	0	1
568	**Can The Can** Suzi Quatro	1973	1	2	1	0	1
569	**Billie Jean** Michael Jackson	1983	1	2	1	0	1
570	**Legend Of Xanadu** Dave Dee, Dozy, Beaky Mick and Tich	1968	1	2	1	0	1
571	**No Charge** J.J. Barrie	1976	1	2	1	0	1
572	**True Blue** Madonna	1986	1	2	1	0	1
573	**Start** Jam	1980	1	2	1	0	1
574	**Jealous Mind** Alvin Stardust	1974	1	2	1	0	1
575	**Show You The Way To Go** Jacksons	1977	1	2	1	0	0

Continued

36 It is March, 1967, Engelbert Humperdinck is number one with 'Release Me' and he is showing Lulu his spare rib.

Above **37** It would be tempting to say that Brotherhood Of Man are shown with the producer and co-writer of 'Save Your Kisses For Me', Tony Hiller, but we'll let sleeping dogs lie. Left **38** Mary Hopkin was seen on the television talent show *Opportunity Knocks* by Twiggy, who recommended her to Paul McCartney, who produced 'Those Were The Days'.

Rank	Title and Artist	Year	No.1	No.2	No.3	No.4	No.5
576	**Fire** Crazy World of Arthur Brown	1968	1	2	1	0	0
577	**There Must Be An Angel (Playing With My Heart)** Eurythmics	1985	1	2	1	0	0
578	**I Should Have Known Better** Jim Diamond	1984	1	2	1	0	0
579	**Uptown Top Ranking** Althia and Donna	1977	1	2	1	0	0
580	**All Or Nothing** Small Faces	1966	1	2	1	0	0
581	**Who's That Girl** Madonna	1987	1	2	1	0	0
582	**Out Of Time** Chris Farlowe and the Thunderbirds	1966	1	2	1	0	0
583	**Tears On My Pillow** Kylie Minogue	1990	1	2	1	0	0
584	**Dreadlock Holiday** 10 C.C.	1978	1	2	0	3	0
585	**A Little Time** Beautiful South	1990	1	2	0	2	0
586	**Ballad Of Bonnie And Clyde** Georgie Fame	1967	1	2	0	1	0
587	**Concrete And Clay** Unit Four Plus Two	1965	1	2	0	1	0
588	**If I Was** Midge Ure	1985	1	2	0	1	0
589	**Let's Party** Jive Bunny and the Mastermixers	1989	1	2	0	1	0
590	**(Just Like) Starting Over** John Lennon	1980	1	2	0	0	2
591	**Voodoo Chile** Jimi Hendrix Experience	1970	1	2	0	0	2
592	**Tired Of Waiting For You** Kinks	1965	1	2	0	0	1
593	**Paint It, Black** Rolling Stones	1966	1	2	0	0	1
594	**Video Killed The Radio Star** Buggles	1979	1	2	0	0	1
595	**Where Are You Now (My Love)** Jackie Trent	1965	1	2	0	0	1
596	**With A Little Help From My Friends** Joe Cocker	1968	1	2	0	0	1
597	**My Camera Never Lies** Bucks Fizz	1982	1	2	0	0	1
598	**The Stonk** Hale and Pace and the Stonkers	1991	1	2	0	0	0
599	**I Pretend** Des O'Connor	1968	1	1	3	0	2
600	**Make It Easy On Yourself** Walker Brothers	1965	1	1	3	0	0
601	**Take Me Bak 'Ome** Slade	1972	1	1	3	0	0
602	**Shakin' All Over** Johnny Kidd and the Pirates	1960	1	1	2	1	1
603	**Diane** Bachelors	1964	1	1	2	1	0
604	**Dizzy** Tommy Roe	1969	1	1	2	1	0
605	**Dance On** Shadows	1962	1	1	2	1	0
606	**Go Now** Moody Blues	1964	1	1	2	1	0
607	**Israelites** Desmond Dekker and the Aces	1969	1	1	2	0	1
608	**Walking On The Moon** Police	1979	1	1	2	0	1
609	**(You're The) Devil In Disguise** Elvis Presley	1963	1	1	2	0	1
610	**Begin The Beguine (Volver a Empezar)** Julio Iglesias	1981	1	1	2	0	0
611	**Angel Fingers** Wizzard	1973	1	1	2	0	0
612	**Saviour's Day** Cliff Richard	1990	1	1	2	0	0
613	**Michael** Highwaymen	1961	1	1	2	0	0
614	**Oh Julie** Shakin' Stevens	1982	1	1	2	0	0
615	**Poor Me** Adam Faith	1960	1	1	1	2	2
616	**Sadness Part 1** Enigma	1990	1	1	1	2	0

Continued

Rank	Title and Artist	Year	No.1	No.2	No.3	No.4	No.5
617	**Float On** Floaters	1977	1	1	1	2	0
618	**Do It Again** Beach Boys	1968	1	1	1	1	1
619	**The Model/Computer Love** Kraftwerk	1981	1	1	1	1	1
620	**The Minute You're Gone** Cliff Richard	1965	1	1	1	1	0
621	**Foot Tapper** Shadows	1963	1	1	1	1	0
622	**Japanese Boy** Aneka	1981	1	1	1	1	0
623	**The Streak** Ray Stevens	1974	1	1	1	1	0
624	**Da Ya Think I'm Sexy** Rod Stewart	1978	1	1	1	1	0
625	**Call Me** Blondie	1980	1	1	1	1	0
626	**Blackberry Way** Move	1968	1	1	1	0	2
627	**Always Yours** Gary Glitter	1974	1	1	1	0	1
628	**Every Little Thing She Does Is Magic** Police	1981	1	1	1	0	0
629	**I've Never Been To Me** Charlene	1982	1	1	1	0	0
630	**D.I.V.O.R.C.E.** Billy Connolly	1975	1	1	1	0	0
631	**Desire** U2	1988	1	1	1	0	0
632	**King Of The Road** Roger Miller	1965	1	1	0	2	1
633	**The Day The Rains Came** Jane Morgan	1958	1	1	0	1	1
634	**Singing The Blues** Tommy Steele	1956	1	1	0	1	0
635	**Ms Grace** Tymes	1974	1	1	0	1	0
636	**You Don't Have To Say You Love Me** Dusty Springfield	1966	1	1	0	1	0
637	**Doctorin' The Tardis** Timelords	1988	1	1	0	1	0
638	**House Of The Rising Sun** Animals	1964	1	1	0	0	1
639	**The Fly** U2	1991	1	1	0	0	1
640	**Innuendo** Queen	1990	1	1	0	0	0
641	**The Roussos Phenomenon EP** Demis Roussos	1976	1	0	3	1	0
642	**Kon-Tiki** Shadows	1961	1	0	2	1	1
643	**Starry Eyed** Michael Holliday	1960	1	0	2	0	2
644	**The Power Of Love** Frankie Goes To Hollywood	1984	1	0	2	0	1
645	**Sad Sweet Dreamer** Sweet Sensation	1974	1	0	2	0	1
646	**Candy Girl** New Edition	1983	1	0	2	0	1
647	**Little Red Rooster** Rolling Stones	1964	1	0	2	0	1
648	**Down Down** Status Quo	1974	1	0	1	0	1
649	**On The Rebound** Floyd Cramer	1961	1	0	1	0	0
650	**Get Away** Georgie Fame and the Blue Flames	1966	1	0	0	2	1
651	**Love Letters In The Sand** Pat Boone	1957	0	7	2	1	2
652	**Are You Sure** Allisons	1961	0	6	2	1	0
653	**Ruby Don't Take Your Love To Town** Kenny Rogers and the First Edition	1969	0	6	1	1	1
654	**The Smurf Song** Father Abraham and the Smurfs	1978	0	6	1	1	0
655	**I'm Too Sexy** Right Said Fred	1991	0	6	1	0	1

Continued

Rank	Title and Artist	Year	Weeks No.1	No.2	No.3	No.4	No.5
656	**The Floral Dance** Brighouse and Rastrick Brass Band	1977	0	6	0	0	1
657	**A Little Bit More** Dr. Hook	1976	0	5	2	0	1
658	**Jeepster** T. Rex	1971	0	5	2	0	0
659	**Don't Forbid Me** Pat Boone	1957	0	5	1	4	1
660	**All Right Now** Free	1970	0	5	1	2	1
661	**As Long As He Needs Me** Shirley Bassey	1960	0	5	1	0	1
662	**Heal The World** Michael Jackson	1992	0	5	1	0	1
663	**Last Christmas/Everything She Wants** Wham!	1984	0	5	1	0	0
664	**Ma He's Making Eyes At Me** Johnny Otis	1957	0	5	0	2	2
665	**Never Ending Song Of Love** New Seekers	1971	0	5	0	1	1
666	**Save The Last Dance For Me** Drifters	1960	0	4	2	0	2
667	**Pushbike Song** Mixtures	1971	0	4	2	0	0
668	**Zambesi** Lou Busch	1956	0	4	1	1	1
669	**Speedy Gonzales** Pat Boone	1962	0	4	1	1	1
670	**I'll Never Fall In Love Again** Tom Jones	1967	0	4	1	1	1
671	**Party** Elvis Presley	1957	0	4	1	1	1
672	**Vienna** Ultravox	1981	0	4	1	1	0
673	**Morningtown Ride** Seekers	1986	0	4	1	1	0
674	**Can't Be With You Tonight** Judy Boucher	1987	0	4	1	1	0
675	**Tom Hark** Elias and his Zigzag Jive Flutes	1958	0	4	1	0	0
676	**The Loco-Motion** Kylie Minogue	1988	0	4	1	0	0
677	**There Goes My Everything** Engelbert Humperdinck	1967	0	4	0	2	0
678	**Let's Dance** Chris Montez	1962	0	4	0	1	1
679	**You Drive Me Crazy** Shakin' Stevens	1981	0	4	0	0	1
680	**Daddy's Home** Cliff Richard	1981	0	4	0	0	0
681	**Got My Mind Set On You** George Harrison	1987	0	4	0	0	0
682	**I Have A Dream** Abba	1979	0	4	0	0	0
683	**Drop The Boy** Bros	1988	0	4	0	0	0
684	**Hound Dog** Elvis Presley	1956	0	3	4	1	2
685	**When I'm Dead And Gone** McGuinness Flint	1970	0	3	4	0	0
686	**Green Door** Frankie Vaughan	1956	0	3	3	3	0
687	**Crazy For You** Madonna	1985	0	3	3	1	1
688	**From A Jack To A King** Ned Miller	1963	0	3	3	1	0
689	**Banana Boat Song** Harry Belafonte	1957	0	3	3	0	1
690	**Please Please Me** Beatles	1963	0	3	3	0	1
691	**Lost John/Stewball** Lonnie Donegan	1956	0	3	3	0	1
692	**I'm Looking Out The Window** Cliff Richard and the Shadows	1962	0	3	2	2	0
693	**Wind Me Up (Let Me Go)** Cliff Richard	1965	0	3	2	1	1
694	**Crazy Horses** Osmonds	1972	0	3	2	1	1
695	**Volare** Dean Martin	1958	0	3	2	1	1
696	**Crackers International EP** Erasure	1988	0	3	2	1	0

Continued

THE UK TOP 1000 SINGLES

Rank	Title and Artist	Year	Weeks				
			No.1	No.2	No.3	No.4	No.5

Rank	Title and Artist	Year	No.1	No.2	No.3	No.4	No.5
697	**American Pie** Don McLean	1972	0	3	2	1	0
698	**Beg Steal Or Borrow** New Seekers	1972	0	3	2	1	0
699	**Tell Me What He Said** Helen Shapiro	1962	0	3	2	0	3
700	**I.O.U.** Freeez	1983	0	3	2	0	1
701	**Informer** Snow	1993	0	3	2	0	1
702	**Mother Of Mine** Neil Reid	1972	0	3	2	0	1
703	**Dance Away** Roxy Music	1979	0	3	2	0	0
704	**On A Ragga Tip** SL2	1992	0	3	2	0	0
705	**When You Come Back To Me** Jason Donovan	1989	0	3	2	0	0
706	**D.I.S.C.O.** Ottowan	1980	0	3	2	0	0
707	**The Trail Of The Lonesome Pine** Laurel and Hardy with the Avalon Boys	1975	0	3	2	0	0
708	**Nessun Dorma** Luciano Pavarotti	1990	0	3	2	0	0
709	**Love Of The Common People** Paul Young	1983	0	3	1	2	2
710	**You Sexy Thing** Hot Chocolate	1975	0	3	1	2	0
711	**A Man Without Love** Engelbert Humperdinck	1968	0	3	1	2	0
712	**Delilah** Tom Jones	1968	0	3	1	1	1
713	**Hello Hello I'm Back Again** Gary Glitter	1973	0	3	1	1	1
714	**Axel F** Harold Faltermeyer	1985	0	3	1	1	1
715	**Oliver's Army** Elvis Costello and the Attractions	1979	0	3	1	1	1
716	**Brown Sugar/Bitch/Let It Rock** Rolling Stones	1971	0	3	1	1	1
717	**Magical Mystery Tour EP** Beatles	1967	0	3	1	1	1
718	**Ghostbusters** Ray Parker Jr	1984	0	3	1	1	0
719	**Love And Pride** King	1985	0	3	1	1	0
720	**Black Is Black** La Belle Epoque	1977	0	3	1	1	0
721	**Sit Down** James	1991	0	3	1	1	0
722	**Part Of The Union** Strawbs	1973	0	3	1	1	0
723	**Against All Odds (Take A Look At Me Now)** Phil Collins	1984	0	3	1	1	0
724	**Patches** Clarence Carter	1970	0	3	1	1	0
725	**Loco-Motion** Little Eva	1962	0	3	1	0	2
726	**Denis** Blondie	1978	0	3	1	0	2
727	**Magic Fly** Space	1977	0	3	1	0	2
728	**Take On Me** A-Ha	1985	0	3	1	0	2
729	**Rock 'N' Roll (Parts 1 And 2)** Gary Glitter	1972	0	3	1	0	1
730	**Goodbye** Mary Hopkin	1969	0	3	1	0	1
731	**The Ballad Of Davy Crockett** Bill Hayes	1956	0	3	1	0	1
732	**Push It/Tramp** Salt-N-Pepa	1988	0	3	1	0	1
733	**Girl I'm Gonna Miss You** Milli Vanilli	1989	0	3	1	0	1
734	**Some Girls** Racey	1979	0	3	1	0	1
735	**My Oh My** Slade	1983	0	3	1	0	1
736	**Tom's Diner** DNA featuring Suzanne Vega	1990	0	3	1	0	1

Continued

Above **39** 'I Hear You Knocking' was a 1955 rhythm & blues smash for Smiley Lewis and a 1970 number one for Dave Edmunds.

Left **41** Elton John and Kiki Dee perform their international number one at the Dr. Pepper Music Festival in New York's Central Park on 2 August, 1977.

THE UK TOP 1000 SINGLES

Rank	Title and Artist	Year	Weeks				
			No.1	No.2	No.3	No.4	No.5

Rank	Title and Artist	Year	No.1	No.2	No.3	No.4	No.5
737	Bridget The Midget (The Queen Of The Blues) Ray Stevens	1971	0	3	1	0	0
738	Ballroom Blitz Sweet	1973	0	3	1	0	0
739	I Can't Let Go Hollies	1966	0	3	1	0	0
740	Witch Queen Of New Orleans Redbone	1971	0	3	1	0	0
741	Je Ne Sais Pas Pourquoi Kylie Minogue	1988	0	3	1	0	0
742	If You Don't Know Me By Now Simply Red	1989	0	3	1	0	0
743	Downtown Petula Clark	1961	0	3	0	3	0
744	In The Ghetto Elvis Presley	1969	0	3	0	2	2
745	Voice In The Wilderness Cliff Richard and the Shadows	1960	0	3	0	2	0
746	Give Peace A Chance John Lennon/Plastic Ono Band	1969	0	3	0	2	0
747	All Night Long (All Night) Lionel Richie	1983	0	3	0	2	0
748	The Living Years Mike and the Mechanics	1989	0	3	0	2	0
749	It's All In The Game Cliff Richard	1963	0	3	0	2	0
750	Cradle Of Love Johnny Preston	1960	0	3	0	1	2
751	No Doubt About It Hot Chocolate	1980	0	3	0	1	1
752	It's My Life Dr. Alban	1992	0	3	0	1	1
753	Come Prima Marino Marini	1958	0	3	0	1	1
754	Hell Raiser Sweet	1973	0	3	0	1	1
755	Let Me In Osmonds	1973	0	3	0	1	1
756	Bits And Pieces Dave Clark Five	1964	0	3	0	1	0
757	Kissin' In The Back Row Of The Movies Drifters	1974	0	3	0	1	0
758	On My Own Patti Labelle and Michael McDonald	1986	0	3	0	1	0
759	Heart Full Of Soul Yardbirds	1965	0	3	0	1	0
760	Teenage Rampage Sweet	1974	0	3	0	1	0
761	Got To Be Certain Kylie Minogue	1988	0	3	0	1	0
762	Exterminate! Snap! featuring Niki Harris	1993	0	3	0	1	0
763	Penny Lane/Strawberry Fields Forever Beatles	1967	0	3	0	0	2
764	Going In With My Eyes Open David Soul	1977	0	3	0	0	2
765	Stranger On The Shore Mr. Acker Bilk with the Leon Young String Chorale	1961	0	3	0	0	1
766	Let 'Em In Wings	1976	0	3	0	0	1
767	Barcelona Freddie Mercury and Montserrat Caballe	1987	0	3	0	0	1
768	Almost There Andy Williams	1965	0	3	0	0	1
769	Hole In My Shoe neil	1984	0	3	0	0	1
770	Children Of The Revolution T. Rex	1972	0	3	0	0	1
771	Happy Birthday Altered Images	1981	0	3	0	0	1
772	We Are The Champions Queen	1977	0	3	0	0	0
773	Love Shack B-52s	1990	0	3	0	0	0

Continued

43 'Get Back' by The Beatles with Billy Preston is the only case in the Fab Four's 17 number ones in which they billed another artist.

44 The Bay City Rollers were (left to right): Derek Longmuir, Stuart 'Woody' Wood, Les McKeown, Alan Longmuir and Eric Faulkner.

THE UK TOP 1000 SINGLES

Rank	Title and Artist	Year	Weeks No.1	No.2	No.3	No.4	No.5

Rank	Title and Artist	Year	No.1	No.2	No.3	No.4	No.5
774	**Son Of Hickory Holler's Tramp** O.C. Smith	1968	0	3	0	0	0
775	**A View To A Kill** Duran Duran	1985	0	3	0	0	0
776	**Holding Out For A Hero** Bonnie Tyler	1985	0	3	0	0	0
777	**Mirror Man** Human League	1982	0	3	0	0	0
778	**Nineteenth Nervous Breakdown** Rolling Stones	1966	0	3	0	0	0
779	**Love Is A Many Splendoured Thing** Four Aces	1955	0	2	5	0	3
780	**Battle Of New Orleans** Lonnie Donegan	1959	0	2	4	3	1
781	**A Mess Of Blues** Elvis Presley	1960	0	2	4	3	0
782	**Honey** Bobby Goldsboro	1968	0	2	4	0	2
783	**A Picture Of You** Joe Brown and the Bruvvers	1962	0	2	3	4	0
784	**Heartbreak Hotel** Elvis Presley	1956	0	2	3	3	1
785	**Let's Twist Again** Chubby Checker	1961	0	2	3	1	2
786	**Last Train To San Fernando** Johnny Duncan and the Bluegrass Boys	1957	0	2	3	1	1
787	**Build Me Up Buttercup** Foundations	1968	0	2	3	0	1
788	**Get Ready For This** 2 Unlimited	1991	0	2	3	0	1
789	**Wake Up Little Susie** Everly Brothers	1957	0	2	3	0	1
790	**Pop Muzik** M	1979	0	2	3	0	1
791	**Saved By The Bell** Robin Gibb	1969	0	2	3	0	1
792	**Funky Town** Lipps Inc	1980	0	2	3	0	0
793	**A Teenager In Love** Marty Wilde	1959	0	2	2	3	1
794	**Agadoo** Black Lace	1984	0	2	2	2	1
795	**Justified And Ancient** KLF featuring Tammy Wynette	1991	0	2	2	2	1
796	**Dream Baby** Roy Orbison	1962	0	2	2	1	1
797	**Everybody Wants To Rule The World** Tears For Fears	1985	0	2	2	1	1
798	**I'm Gonna Be Strong** Gene Pitney	1964	0	2	2	1	0
799	**Under The Boardwalk** Bruce Willis	1987	0	2	2	1	0
800	**Do You Want To Know A Secret** Billy J. Kramer and the Dakotas	1963	0	2	2	1	0
801	**Substitute** Clout	1978	0	2	2	1	0
802	**Eloise** Barry Ryan	1968	0	2	2	1	0
803	**Get Up (Before The Night Is Over)** Technotronic featuring Ya Kid K	1990	0	2	2	1	0
804	**God Only Knows** Beach Boys	1966	0	2	2	0	2
805	**Co Co** Sweet	1971	0	2	2	0	2
806	**Black Night** Deep Purple	1970	0	2	2	0	2
807	**Do You Want To Touch Me? (Oh Yeah)** Gary Glitter	1971	0	2	2	0	1
808	**So Macho/Cruising** Sinitta	1986	0	2	2	0	1

Continued

Rank	Title and Artist	Year	No.1	No.2	No.3	No.4	No.5
809	**Hooked On Classics** Royal Philharmonic Orchestra conducted by Louis Clark	1981	0	2	2	0	1
810	**Waterloo Sunset** Kinks	1967	0	2	2	0	1
811	**My Girl** Temptations	1965	0	2	2	0	1
812	**Neanderthal Man** Hotlegs	1970	0	2	2	0	0
813	**Can't Get By Without You** Real Thing	1976	0	2	2	0	0
814	**We Don't Have To...** Jermaine Stewart	1986	0	2	2	0	0
815	**Silly Games** Janet Kay	1979	0	2	2	0	0
816	**I Love Your Smile** Shanice	1992	0	2	2	0	0
817	**Black Velvet** Alannah Myles	1990	0	2	2	0	0
818	**Love Changes Everything** Michael Ball	1989	0	2	2	0	0
819	**Say Say Say** Paul McCartney and Michael Jackson	1983	0	2	2	0	0
820	**Donna** 10 C.C.	1972	0	2	2	0	0
821	**Everybody Knows** Dave Clark Five	1967	0	2	2	0	0
822	**Another Day** Paul McCartney	1971	0	2	1	2	1
823	**Hello Mary Lou/Travellin' Man** Ricky Nelson	1961	0	2	1	2	0
824	**Oh Well** Fleetwood Mac	1969	0	2	1	2	0
825	**When You Tell Me That You Love Me** Diana Ross	1991	0	2	1	2	0
826	**Atlantis** Shadows	1963	0	2	1	2	0
827	**Someone Someone** Brian Poole and the Tremeloes	1964	0	2	1	2	0
828	**Pump Up The Jam** Technotronic featuring Felly	1989	0	2	1	2	0
829	**Big Man** Four Preps	1958	0	2	1	1	2
830	**Flowers In The Rain** Move	1967	0	2	1	1	1
831	**Dance Yourself Dizzy** Liquid Gold	1980	0	2	1	1	1
832	**Then He Kissed Me** Crystals	1963	0	2	1	1	1
833	**Chi Mai (Theme From 'The Life & Times Of David Lloyd George')** Ennio Morricone	1981	0	2	1	1	1
834	**(Call Me) Number One** Tremeloes	1969	0	2	1	1	0
835	**Golden Brown** Stranglers	1982	0	2	1	1	0
836	**There's A Whole Lot Of Lovin'** Guys and Dolls	1975	0	2	1	1	0
837	**Kids In America** Kim Wilde	1981	0	2	1	1	0
838	**The Twist (Yo, Twist)** Fat Boys and Chubby Checker	1988	0	2	1	1	0
839	**More Than Words** Extreme	1991	0	2	1	1	0
840	**Let's Talk About Sex** Salt-N-Pepa	1991	0	2	1	1	0
841	**Rasputin** Boney M	1978	0	2	1	1	0
842	**Last Train To Trancentral** KLF featuring the Children Of The Revolution	1991	0	2	1	1	0
843	**Rain Or Shine** Five Star	1986	0	2	1	1	0
844	**Loving You** Minnie Riperton	1975	0	2	1	1	0
845	**You Can Get It If You Really Want** Desmond Dekker	1970	0	2	1	1	0

Continued

Left **45** When Mickey Finn (top) replaced Steve Took, Marc Bolan's act Tyrannosaurus Rex became T. Rex and had eight consecutive top two monsters.

46 Appropriately enough, the highest-placed of the eleven Abba hits in the Top 1000 returned for a second top twenty run in 1992.

Rank	Title and Artist	Year	No.1	No.2	No.3	No.4	No.5
846	Groove Is In The Heart/What Is Love Deee-Lite	1990	0	2	1	1	0
847	Abracadabra Steve Miller Band	1982	0	2	1	1	0
848	This Town Ain't Big Enough For Both Of Us Sparks	1974	0	2	1	1	0
849	Joanna/Tonight Kool and the Gang	1984	0	2	1	1	0
850	Hopelessly Devoted To You Olivia Newton-John	1978	0	2	1	1	0
851	Back Off Boogaloo Ringo Starr	1972	0	2	1	1	0
852	My Generation Who	1965	0	2	1	0	2
853	Bad Boys Wham!	1983	0	2	1	0	2
854	Killer Queen Queen	1974	0	2	1	0	2
855	When Forever Has Gone Demis Roussos	1976	0	2	1	0	2
856	You Ain't Seen Nothing Yet Bachman-Turner Overdrive	1974	0	2	1	0	1
857	I'm Telling You Now Freddie and the Dreamers	1963	0	2	1	0	1
858	Better The Devil You Know Kylie Minogue	1989	0	2	1	0	1
859	Far Far Away Slade	1974	0	2	1	0	1
860	Birdie Song (Birdie Dance) Tweets	1981	0	2	1	0	1
861	Upside Down Diana Ross	1980	0	2	1	0	1
862	Crazy Little Thing Called Love Queen	1979	0	2	1	0	1
863	Chiquitita Abba	1979	0	2	1	0	1
864	The Harder I Try Brother Beyond	1988	0	2	1	0	1
865	Heartbreaker Dionne Warwick	1982	0	2	1	0	1
866	Beat Dis Bomb The Bass	1988	0	2	1	0	1
867	Oh Happy Day Edwin Hawkins Singers	1969	0	2	1	0	1
868	Matthew And Son Cat Stevens	1967	0	2	1	0	1
869	They Don't Know Tracey Ullman	1983	0	2	1	0	1
870	Fox On The Run Sweet	1975	0	2	1	0	1
871	Wind Of Change Scorpions	1991	0	2	1	0	1
872	Mickey Toni Basil	1982	0	2	1	0	1
873	Right Here Waiting Richard Marx	1989	0	2	1	0	1
874	Bend It Dave Dee, Dozy, Beaky, Mick and Tich	1966	0	2	1	0	0
875	I Did What I Did For Maria Tony Christie	1971	0	2	1	0	0
876	Don't Know Much Linda Ronstadt with Aaron Neville	1989	0	2	1	0	0
877	You Keep Me Hangin' On Kim Wilde	1986	0	2	1	0	0
878	A Love Worth Waiting For Shakin' Stevens	1984	0	2	1	0	0
879	Red Light Spells Danger Billy Ocean	1977	0	2	1	0	0
880	Wouldn't Change A Thing Kylie Minogue	1989	0	2	1	0	0
881	Daydream Lovin' Spoonful	1966	0	2	1	0	0
882	Gold Spandau Ballet	1983	0	2	1	0	0
883	Full Metal Jacket (I Wanna Be Your Drill Instructor) Abigail Mead and Nigel Goulding	1987	0	2	1	0	0

Continued

Rank	Title and Artist	Year	Weeks No.1	No.2	No.3	No.4	No.5
884	Let's Hear It For The Boy Deniece Williams	1984	0	2	1	0	0
885	What Have I Done To Deserve This Pet Shop Boys with Dusty Springfield	1987	0	2	1	0	0
886	The Cat Crept In Mud	1974	0	2	1	0	0
887	Excerpt From 'A Teenage Opera' Keith West	1967	0	2	0	3	1
888	To Know Him Is To Love Him Teddy Bears	1958	0	2	0	2	1
889	Yesterday Once More Carpenters	1973	0	2	0	2	1
890	Automatic Pointer Sisters	1984	0	2	0	2	1
891	Streets Of London Ralph McTell	1974	0	2	0	2	0
892	Antmusic Adam and the Ants	1980	0	2	0	2	0
893	The Best Things In Life Are Free Luther Vandross and Janet Jackson	1992	0	2	0	2	0
894	I'm The One Gerry and the Pacemakers	1964	0	2	0	2	0
895	Hard Headed Woman Elvis Presley	1958	0	2	0	2	0
896	You See The Trouble With Me Barry White	1976	0	2	0	2	0
897	Radio Ga Ga Queen	1984	0	2	0	2	0
898	(Dancing On) A Saturday Night Barry Blue	1973	0	2	0	2	0
899	Words F.R. David	1983	0	2	0	2	0
900	When A Man Loves A Woman Percy Sledge	1966	0	2	0	1	2
901	Seaside Shuffle Terry Dactyl and the Dinosaurs	1972	0	2	0	1	2
902	Rag Doll Four Seasons	1964	0	2	0	1	2
903	What You're Proposin' Status Quo	1980	0	2	0	1	2
904	My Sentimental Friend Herman's Hermits	1969	0	2	0	1	1
905	Glass Of Champagne Sailor	1975	0	2	0	1	1
906	Love Don't Live Here Anymore Rose Royce	1978	0	2	0	1	1
907	One Day I'll Fly Away Randy Crawford	1980	0	2	0	1	1
908	Stars On 45 (Volume 2) Starsound	1981	0	2	0	1	1
909	Four Bacharach And David Songs EP Deacon Blue	1990	0	2	0	1	1
910	Heartache Pepsi and Shirlie	1987	0	2	0	1	0
911	Holding Back The Years Simply Red	1985	0	2	0	1	0
912	That Ole Devil Called Love Alison Moyet	1985	0	2	0	1	0
913	Stop Stop Stop Hollies	1966	0	2	0	1	0
914	Heartbeat Nick Berry	1992	0	2	0	1	0
915	When I Fall In Love/My Arms Keep Missing You Rick Astley	1987	0	2	0	1	0
916	The Shakin' Stevens EP Shakin' Stevens	1982	0	2	0	1	0
917	In The Navy Village People	1979	0	2	0	1	0
918	Fairytale Of New York Pogues featuring Kirsty MacColl	1987	0	2	0	1	0
919	Together Forever Rick Astley	1988	0	2	0	1	0
920	Welcome To The Pleasuredome Frankie Goes To Hollywood	1985	0	2	0	0	2
921	Wild Wind John Leyton	1961	0	2	0	0	1
922	All Day And All Of The Night Kinks	1964	0	2	0	0	1
923	Church Of The Poison Mind Culture Club	1983	0	2	0	0	1

Continued

Above **48** Culture Club had seven consecutive UK and six straight US top ten hits. Left **47** 'Band Of Gold' by Freda Payne was produced by Holland-Dozier-Holland. In the mid-70s Freda's sister Scherrie joined the Supremes, who had originally become famous with Holland-Dozier-Holland material. Below **49** Though his erstwhile partner Paul Simon had more success in the album charts, Art Garfunkel had two number one solo singles, Simon and Garfunkel had one, and Simon alone had none.

THE UK TOP 1000 SINGLES

Rank	Title and Artist	Year	Weeks				
			No.1	No.2	No.3	No.4	No.5

Rank	Title and Artist	Year	No.1	No.2	No.3	No.4	No.5
924	**Faith** George Michael	1987	0	2	0	0	1
925	**The Bitterest Pill (I Ever Had To Swallow)** Jam	1982	0	2	0	0	1
926	**I'll Be There** Mariah Carey	1992	0	2	0	0	1
927	**Be My Girl** Jim Dale	1957	0	2	0	0	0
928	**With You I'm Born Again** Billy Preston and Syreeta	1979	0	2	0	0	0
929	**The Best Of Me** Cliff Richard	1989	0	2	0	0	0
930	**The Brits 1990** Various Artists	1990	0	2	0	0	0
931	**Why Can't I Wake Up With You** Take That	1993	0	2	0	0	0
932	**When I Fall In Love** Nat 'King' Cole	1957	0	1	4	3	0
933	**Return To Me** Dean Martin	1958	0	1	4	2	1
934	**Baker Street** Undercover	1992	0	1	4	1	1
935	**I Believe** Bachelors	1964	0	1	4	1	0
936	**Hippy Hippy Shake** Swinging Blue Jeans	1963	0	1	4	1	0
937	**The Last Farewell** Roger Whittaker	1975	0	1	4	0	1
938	**Jesamine** Casuals	1968	0	1	4	0	0
939	**Stars On 45** Starsound	1981	0	1	4	0	0
940	**Walk Hand In Hand** Tony Martin	1956	0	1	3	2	1
941	**Tammy** Debbie Reynolds	1957	0	1	3	2	0
942	**Fanfare For The Common Man** Emerson Lake and Palmer	1977	0	1	3	1	1
943	**Swiss Maid** Del Shannon	1962	0	1	3	1	0
944	**Big Bad John** Jimmy Dean	1961	0	1	3	1	0
945	**Groovin' With Mr. Bloe** Mr. Bloe	1970	0	1	3	1	0
946	**Solid Gold Easy Action** T. Rex	1972	0	1	3	1	0
947	**What Would I Be** Val Doonican	1966	0	1	3	1	0
948	**Man Of The World** Fleetwood Mac	1969	0	1	3	1	0
949	**The Air That I Breathe** Hollies	1974	0	1	3	1	0
950	**Boy From New York City** Darts	1978	0	1	3	1	0
951	**Bird Dog** Everly Brothers	1958	0	1	3	0	2
952	**My Boy Lollipop** Millie	1964	0	1	3	0	2
953	**Did You Ever** Nancy and Lee	1971	0	1	3	0	1
954	**Someone Else's Baby** Adam Faith	1960	0	1	3	0	1
955	**Three Steps To Heaven** Showaddywaddy	1975	0	1	3	0	1
956	**Dedicated To The One I Love** Mamas and the Papas	1967	0	1	3	0	0
957	**You Make Me Feel Like Dancing** Leo Sayer	1976	0	1	3	0	0
958	**Indiana Wants Me** R. Dean Taylor	1971	0	1	3	0	0
959	**Bang Bang** B. A. Robertson	1979	0	1	3	0	0
960	**Let's Work Together** Canned Heat	1970	0	1	3	0	0
961	**You've Got Your Troubles** Fortunes	1965	0	1	3	0	0
962	**I'm Gonna Make You Mine** Lou Christie	1969	0	1	3	0	0
963	**Torch** Soft Cell	1982	0	1	3	0	0
964	**I Believe In Father Christmas** Greg Lake	1975	0	1	3	0	0

Continued

THE UK TOP 1000 SINGLES

			Weeks				
Rank	Title and Artist	Year	No.1	No.2	No.3	No.4	No.5

965	**Lola** Kinks	1970	0	1	2	3	1
966	**Tweedle Dee Tweedle Dum** Middle Of The Road	1971	0	1	2	3	0
967	**Because They're Young** Duane Eddy	1960	0	1	2	2	1
968	**Mama/Robot Man** Connie Francis	1960	0	1	2	2	0
969	**Come Back My Love** Darts	1978	0	1	2	2	0
970	**Sandy** John Travolta	1978	0	1	2	2	0
971	**It's Raining** Darts	1978	0	1	2	2	0
972	**Things** Bobby Darin	1962	0	1	2	1	2
973	**Ma Baker** Boney M	1977	0	1	2	1	2
974	**Dirty Cash** Adventures Of Stevie V	1990	0	1	2	1	2
975	**Hey Rock And Roll** Showaddywaddy	1974	0	1	2	1	1
976	**Scarlett O'Hara** Jet Harris and Tony Meehan	1963	0	1	2	1	1
977	**Miss You Like Crazy** Natalie Cole	1989	0	1	2	1	1
978	**We Will Make Love** Russ Hamilton	1957	0	1	2	1	1
979	**Alternate Title** Monkees	1967	0	1	2	1	1
980	**Hole In My Shoe** Traffic	1967	0	1	2	1	1
981	**Sylvia's Mother** Dr. Hook and The Medicine Show	1972	0	1	2	1	1
982	**I'm A Boy** Who	1966	0	1	2	1	1
983	**Love Really Hurts Without You** Billy Ocean	1976	0	1	2	1	1
984	**Ain't Gonna Bump No More (With No Big Fat Woman)** Joe Tex	1977	0	1	2	1	1
985	**(I Wanna Give You) Devotion** Nomad featuring MC Mikee Freedom	1991	0	1	2	1	1
986	**The Jean Genie** David Bowie	1972	0	1	2	1	1
987	**A Groovy Kind Of Love** Mindbenders	1966	0	1	2	1	0
988	**Boogie Nights** Heatwave	1977	0	1	2	1	0
989	**You Make Me Feel Brand New** Stylistics	1974	0	1	2	1	0
990	**The Price Of Love** Everly Brothers	1965	0	1	2	1	0
991	**Question** Moody Blues	1970	0	1	2	1	0
992	**Hold Me Now** Johnny Logan	1987	0	1	2	1	0
993	**The Show Must Go On** Leo Sayer	1973	0	1	2	1	0
994	**Could It Be Forever/Cherish** David Cassidy	1972	0	1	2	1	0
995	**Mona** Craig McLachlan and Check 1-2	1990	0	1	2	1	0
996	**Convoy** C.W. McCall	1976	0	1	2	1	0
997	**London Nights** London Boys	1989	0	1	2	1	0
998	**Sesame's Treet** Smart E's	1992	0	1	2	1	0
999	**Zoom** Fat Larry's Band	1982	0	1	2	1	0
1000	**My Frend Stan** Slade	1973	0	1	2	1	0

50 Ronnie Hilton brings up the rear of the list of illustrated artists who recorded the top 50 singles. He reached number one in 1956 with a Rodgers and Hammerstein song Perry Como had taken to the top in America three years earlier.

PART TWO

YEAR BY
YEAR
TOP 40
CHARTS

A RANKING OF THE
TOP 40 HITS FOR
EACH YEAR

1955: What is called "the rock era" is dated from when 'Rock Around The Clock' by Bill Haley and his Comets reached number one in 1955.

1955 TOP 5

No	Title	Artist
1	**Rock Around The Clock**..................	Bill Haley and his Comets
2	**Christmas Alphabet**...........................	Dickie Valentine
3	**Love Is A Many Splendoured Thing**..	Four Aces
4	**Let's Have A Ding Dong**..................	Winifred Atwell
5	**Meet Me On The Corner**..................	Max Bygraves

1956: Her two American number ones, 'Music! Music! Music!' and 'Till I Waltz Again With You', predated the British chart, but Teresa Brewer still managed two UK top three hits in 1956. Her duet that year with New York Yankees baseball star Mickey Mantle, 'I Love Mickey', was not a hit.

1956 TOP 40

No	Title	Artist
1	Just Walkin' In The Rain	Johnnie Ray
2	Whatever Will Be Will Be	Doris Day
3	No Other Love	Ronnie Hilton
4	I'll Be Home	Pat Boone
5	Woman In Love	Frankie Laine
6	Lay Down Your Arms	Anne Shelton
7	Sixteen Tons	Tennessee Ernie Ford
8	Memories Are Made Of This	Dean Martin
9	Poor People Of Paris	Winifred Atwell
10	Why Do Fools Fall In Love	Teenagers featuring Frankie Lymon
11	It's Almost Tomorrow	Dreamweavers
12	Rock Around The Clock	Bill Haley and his Comets
13	Rock And Roll Waltz	Kay Starr
14	Zambesi	Lou Busch
15	Hound Dog	Elvis Presley
16	Lost John/Stewball	Lonnie Donegan
17	Green Door	Frankie Vaughan
18	Ballad Of Davy Crockett	Bill Hayes
19	Heartbreak Hotel	Elvis Presley
20	Walk Hand In Hand	Tony Martin
21	The Tender Trap	Frank Sinatra
22	All Star Hit Parade	Winifred Atwell/Dave King/Joan Regan/Lita Roza/Dickie Valentine/David Whitfield
23	A Tear Fell	Teresa Brewer
24	Singing The Blues	Guy Mitchell
25	Meet Me On The Corner	Max Bygraves
26	Sweet Old Fashioned Girl	Teresa Brewer
27	St. Therese Of The Roses	Malcolm Vaughan
28	Love Is A Many Splendoured Thing	Four Aces
29	Only You	Hilltoppers
30	Rockin' Through The Rye	Bill Haley and his Comets
31	Love And Marriage	Frank Sinatra
32	Bloodnok's Rock 'n' Roll/Ying Tong Song	Goons
33	My September Love	David Whitfield
34	Ballad Of Davy Crockett	Tennessee Ernie Ford
35	My Prayer	Platters
36	Rock-A-Beatin' Boogie	Bill Haley and his Comets
37	Rip It Up	Bill Haley and his Comets
38	Giddy-Up-A-Ding-Dong	Freddie Bell and the Bellboys
39	More	Jimmy Young
40	Mountain Greenery	Mel Torme

1957 TOP 40

No	Title	Artist
1	Diana	Paul Anka
2	Young Love	Tab Hunter
3	All Shook Up	Elvis Presley
4	Mary's Boy Child	Harry Belafonte
5	Cumberland Gap	Lonnie Donegan
6	Garden Of Eden	Frankie Vaughan
7	Singing The Blues	Guy Mitchell
8	Yes Tonight Josephine	Johnnie Ray
9	That'll Be The Day	Crickets
10	Gamblin' Man/Puttin' On The Style	Lonnie Donegan
11	Butterfly	Andy Williams
12	Rock-A-Billy	Guy Mitchell
13	Singing The Blues	Tommy Steele
14	Love Letters In The Sand	Pat Boone
15	Don't Forbid Me	Pat Boone
16	Party	Elvis Presley
17	Banana Boat Song	Harry Belafonte
18	Last Train To San Fernando	Johnny Duncan and the Bluegrass Boys
19	Ma He's Making Eyes At Me	Johnny Otis Show
20	Be My Girl	Jim Dale
21	When I Fall In Love	Nat 'King' Cole
22	Tammy	Debbie Reynolds
23	We Will Make Love	Russ Hamilton
24	Wake Up Little Susie	Everly Brothers
25	Just Walkin' In The Rain	Johnnie Ray
26	Knee Deep In The Blues	Guy Mitchell
27	Friendly Persuasion	Pat Boone
28	Little Darlin'	Diamonds
29	Teddy Bear	Elvis Presley
30	Island In The Sun	Harry Belafonte
31	Long Tall Sally	Little Richard
32	I Love You Baby	Paul Anka
33	St. Therese Of The Roses	Malcolm Vaughan
34	Green Door	Frankie Vaughan
35	My Special Angel	Malcolm Vaughan
36	Around The World	Ronnie Hilton
37	Don't You Rock Me Daddy-O	Lonnie Donegan
38	True Love	Bing Crosby and Grace Kelly
39	Baby Baby	Frankie Lymon and the Teenagers
40	With All My Heart	Petula Clark

Left **1957**: 'Butterfly' was his only solo number one, but Andy Williams first appeared on an American number one with the Williams Brothers Quartet backing Bing Crosby on the 1944 original of 'Swinging On A Star'.

Below **1958**: The 19-year-old Kalin Twins (Herbie, left, and Harold) of 'When' fame had a top twenty follow-up in America. 'Forget Me Not'. British fans ignored this plea, and the brothers were one-hit wonders in the UK.

1958 TOP 40

No	Title	Artist
1	Magic Moments	Perry Como
2	All I Have To Do Is Dream/ Claudette	Everly Brothers
3	Who's Sorry Now	Connie Francis
4	Carolina Moon/Stupid Cupid	Connie Francis
5	When	Kalin Twins
6	Whole Lotta Woman	Marvin Rainwater
7	Hoots Mon	Lord Rockingham's XI
8	Jailhouse Rock	Elvis Presley
9	It's All In The Game	Tommy Edwards
10	The Story Of My Life	Michael Holliday
11	On The Street Where You Live	Vic Damone
12	It's Only Make Believe	Conway Twitty
13	Great Balls Of Fire	Jerry Lee Lewis
14	Mary's Boy Child	Harry Belafonte
15	Tom Hark	Elias and his Zigzag Jive Flutes
16	Volare	Dean Martin
17	Come Prima	Marino Marini
18	Ma He's Making Eyes At Me	Johnny Otis Show
19	Big Man	Four Preps
20	Hard Headed Woman	Elvis Presley
21	Return To Me	Dean Martin
22	Bird Dog	Everly Brothers
23	A Wonderful Time Up There	Pat Boone
24	Wake Up Little Susie	Everly Brothers
25	Move It	Cliff Richard
26	Lollipop	Mudlarks
27	King Creole	Elvis Presley
28	Don't	Elvis Presley
29	Tom Dooley	Lonnie Donegan
30	You Need Hands/Tulips From Amsterdam	Max Bygraves
31	Swingin' Shepherd Blues	Ted Heath
32	Oh Boy	Crickets
33	All The Way	Frank Sinatra
34	Nairobi	Tommy Steele
35	At The Hop	Danny and the Juniors
36	Wear My Ring Around Your Neck	Elvis Presley
37	My Special Angel	Malcolm Vaughan
38	Stairway Of Love	Michael Holliday
39	Twilight Time	Platters
40	A Certain Smile	Johnny Mathis

Above **1959**: Harold Jenkins changed his name to Conway Twitty, had more number ones than any other act in country music history and subsequently opened a tourist attraction in the USA called Twitty City. He died in 1993. Left **1960**: If nine weeks at number one in America and one week at two in Britain for 'Theme From "A Summer Place"' by the Canadian orchestra leader Percy Faith seems an unbalanced fate, consider the fortune of his 1953 release 'Song From "Moulin Rouge"': ten weeks at number one in the US and no entry at all in the UK.

1959 TOP 40

No	Title	Artist
1	**Living Doll**	Cliff Richard and the Drifters
2	**A Fool Such As I/Need Your Love Tonight**	Elvis Presley
3	**Travellin' Light**	Cliff Richard and the Shadows
4	**Dream Lover**	Bobby Darin
5	**Only Sixteen**	Craig Douglas
6	**As I Love You**	Shirley Bassey
7	**Side Saddle**	Russ Conway
8	**It Doesn't Matter Anymore**	Buddy Holly
9	**One Night/I Got Stung**	Elvis Presley
10	**What Do You Want**	Adam Faith
11	**It's Only Make Believe**	Conway Twitty
12	**Mack The Knife**	Bobby Darin
13	**What Do You Want To Make Those Eyes At Me For**	Emile Ford and the Checkmates
14	**Roulette**	Russ Conway
15	**Smoke Gets In Your Eyes**	Platters
16	**Here Comes Summer**	Jerry Keller
17	**The Day The Rains Came**	Jane Morgan
18	**Battle Of New Orleans**	Lonnie Donegan
19	**A Teenager In Love**	Marty Wilde
20	**Hoots Mon**	Lord Rockingham's XI
21	**To Know Him Is To Love Him**	Teddy Bears
22	**Baby Face**	Little Richard
23	**('Til) I Kissed You**	Everly Brothers
24	**Lonely Boy**	Paul Anka
25	**Petite Fleur**	Chris Barber's Jazz Band
26	**It's Late**	Ricky Nelson
27	**Oh Carol**	Neil Sedaka
28	**Kiss Me Honey Honey Kiss Me**	Shirley Bassey
29	**Sea Of Love**	Marty Wilde
30	**A Pub With No Beer**	Slim Dusty
31	**Red River Rock**	Johnny and the Hurricanes
32	**Lipstick On Your Collar**	Connie Francis
33	**Does Your Chewing Gum Lose Its Flavour**	Lonnie Donegan
34	**Tom Dooley**	Lonnie Donegan
35	**Donna**	Marty Wilde
36	**I've Waited So Long**	Anthony Newley
37	**Tea For Two Cha Cha**	Tommy Dorsey Orchestra starring Warren Covington
38	**My Happiness**	Connie Francis
39	**Seven Little Girls Sitting In The Back Seat**	Avons
40	**A Big Hunk O' Love**	Elvis Presley

1960 TOP 40

No	Title	Artist
1	It's Now Or Never	Elvis Presley
2	Cathy's Clown	Everly Brothers
3	Apache	Shadows
4	Why	Anthony Newley
5	My Old Man's A Dustman	Lonnie Donegan
6	What Do You Want To Make Those Eyes At Me For	Emile Ford and the Checkmates
7	Please Don't Tease	Cliff Richard and the Shadows
8	Good Timin'	Jimmy Jones
9	Tell Laura I Love Her	Ricky Valance
10	Only The Lonely	Roy Orbison
11	Three Steps To Heaven	Eddie Cochran
12	Running Bear	Johnny Preston
13	Do You Mind	Anthony Newley
14	Shakin' All Over	Johnny Kidd and the Pirates
15	Poor Me	Adam Faith
16	I Love You	Cliff Richard and the Shadows
17	Starry Eyed	Michael Holliday
18	As Long As He Needs Me	Shirley Bassey
19	Save The Last Dance For Me	Drifters
20	Voice In The Wilderness	Cliff Richard and the Shadows
21	Cradle Of Love	Johnny Preston
22	What Do You Want	Adam Faith
23	A Mess Of Blues	Elvis Presley
24	Someone Else's Baby	Adam Faith
25	Because They're Young	Duane Eddy
26	Mama/Robot Man	Connie Francis
27	Fall In Love With You	Cliff Richard
28	Theme From 'A Summer Place'	Percy Faith Orchestra
29	Handy Man	Jimmy Jones
30	Rocking Goose	Johnny and the Hurricanes
31	Way Down Yonder In New Orleans	Freddy Cannon
32	Delaware	Perry Como
33	Oh Carol	Neil Sedaka
34	Nine Times Out Of Ten	Cliff Richard and the Shadows
35	Strawberry Fair	Anthony Newley
36	Ain't Misbehaving	Tommy Bruce
37	Little Donkey	Nina and Frederick
38	Seven Little Girls Sitting In The Back Seat	Avons
39	On A Slow Boat To China	Emile Ford and the Checkmates
40	Stuck On You	Elvis Presley

1961 TOP 40

No	Title	Artist
1	Wooden Heart	Elvis Presley
2	Johnny Remember Me	John Leyton
3	Are You Lonesome Tonight	Elvis Presley
4	Little Sister/His Latest Flame	Elvis Presley
5	Surrender	Elvis Presley
6	Runaway	Del Shannon
7	You Don't Know	Helen Shapiro
8	Walkin' Back To Happiness	Helen Shapiro
9	Tower Of Strength	Frankie Vaughan
10	Walk Right Back/Ebony Eyes	Everly Brothers
11	Poetry In Motion	Johnny Tillotson
12	Blue Moon	Marcels
13	Temptation	Everly Brothers
14	Sailor	Petula Clark
15	Reach For The Stars/Climb Ev'ry Mountain	Shirley Bassey
16	Well I Ask You	Eden Kane
17	You're Driving Me Crazy	Temperance Seven
18	Moon River	Danny Williams
19	I Love You	Cliff Richard and the Shadows
20	Michael	Highwaymen
21	Kon–Tiki	Shadows
22	On The Rebound	Floyd Cramer
23	Are You Sure	Allisons
24	Hello Mary Lou/Travellin' Man	Ricky Nelson
25	Wild Wind	John Leyton
26	Big Bad John	Jimmy Dean
27	Save The Last Dance For Me	Drifters
28	Lazy River	Bobby Darin
29	Jealousy	Billy Fury
30	Pepe	Duane Eddy
31	Theme For A Dream	Cliff Richard and the Shadows
32	Frightened City	Shadows
33	Halfway To Paradise	Billy Fury
34	When The Girl In Your Arms Is The Girl In Your Heart	Cliff Richard
35	Take Good Care Of My Baby	Bobby Vee
36	Portrait Of My Love	Matt Monro
37	Romeo	Petula Clark
38	You're Sixteen	Johnny Burnette
39	A Girl Like You	Cliff Richard and the Shadows
40	But I Do	Clarence 'Frogman' Henry

Above **1961**: 'Johnny Remember Me' by John Leyton was the only single not by Elvis Presley in the top five of 1961. Left **1962**: Brenda Lee represents all artists who have hits in the yearly top 40s but none in the all-time Top 1000.

1962 TOP 40

No	Title	Artist
1	Wonderful Land	Shadows
2	I Remember You	Frank Ifield
3	The Young Ones	Cliff Richard and the Shadows
4	Good Luck Charm	Elvis Presley
5	Lovesick Blues	Frank Ifield
6	Telstar	Tornados
7	Rock-A-Hula Baby/Can't Help Falling In Love	Elvis Presley
8	She's Not You	Elvis Presley
9	Return To Sender	Elvis Presley
10	I Can't Stop Loving You	Ray Charles
11	Come Outside	Mike Sarne with Wendy Richard
12	Nut Rocker	B. Bumble and the Stingers
13	Moon River	Danny Williams
14	Speedy Gonzales	Pat Boone
15	Let's Dance	Chris Montez
16	I'm Looking Out The Window/Do You Wanna Dance	Cliff Richard and the Shadows
17	Tell Me What He Said	Helen Shapiro
18	Loco-Motion	Little Eva
19	Stranger On The Shore	Mr. Acker Bilk w.th The Leon Young String Chorale
20	A Picture Of You	Joe Brown and the Bruvvers
21	Let's Twist Again	Chubby Checker
22	Dream Baby	Roy Orbison
23	The Next Time/Bachelor Boy	Cliff Richard and the Shadows
24	Swiss Maid	Del Shannon
25	Things	Bobby Darin
26	It'll Be Me	Cliff Richard and the Shadows
27	Hey! Baby	Bruce Channel
28	Hey Little Girl	Del Shannon
29	Midnight In Moscow	Kenny Ball and his Jazzmen
30	Forget Me Not	Eden Kane
31	Let There Be Drums	Sandy Nelson
32	Sheila	Tommy Roe
33	Happy Birthday Sweet Sixteen	Neil Sedaka
34	Roses Are Red	Ronnie Carroll
35	Bobby's Girl	Susan Maughan
36	It Might As Well Rain Until September	Carole King
37	Sun Arise	Rolf Harris
38	Sealed With A Kiss	Brian Hyland
39	Speak To Me Pretty	Brenda Lee
40	Dance On	Shadows

1963 TOP 40

No	Title	Artist
1	From Me To You	Beatles
2	She Loves You	Beatles
3	You'll Never Walk Alone	Gerry and the Pacemakers
4	I Like It	Gerry and the Pacemakers
5	How Do You Do It	Gerry and the Pacemakers
6	The Next Time/Bachelor Boy	Cliff Richard and the Shadows
7	Summer Holiday	Cliff Richard and the Shadows
8	Do You Love Me	Brian Poole and the Tremeloes
9	Wayward Wind	Frank Ifield
10	Bad To Me	Billy J. Kramer and the Dakotas
11	Diamonds	Jet Harris and Tony Meehan
12	I Want To Hold Your Hand	Beatles
13	Confessin'	Frank Ifield
14	Sweets For My Sweet	Searchers
15	(You're The) Devil In Disguise	Elvis Presley
16	Foot Tapper	Shadows
17	Dance On	Shadows
18	From A Jack To A King	Ned Miller
19	Please Please Me	Beatles
20	It's All In The Game	Cliff Richard
21	Do You Want To Know A Secret	Billy J. Kramer and the Dakotas
22	Atlantis	Shadows
23	Then He Kissed Me	Crystals
24	I'm Telling You Now	Freddie and the Dreamers
25	Return To Sender	Elvis Presley
26	Scarlett O'Hara	Jet Harris and Tony Meehan
27	Sugar And Spice	Searchers
28	Don't Talk To Him	Cliff Richard
29	Can't Get Used To Losing You	Andy Williams
30	You Were Made For Me	Freddie and the Dreamers
31	If You Gotta Make A Fool Of Somebody	Freddie and the Dreamers
32	Like I Do	Maureen Evans
33	That's What Love Will Do	Joe Brown and the Bruvvers
34	Blue Bayou/Mean Woman Blues	Roy Orbison
35	Like I've Never Been Gone	Billy Fury
36	The Night Has A Thousand Eyes	Bobby Vee
37	When Will You Say I Love You	Billy Fury
38	Lovesick Blues	Frank Ifield
39	I Want To Stay Here	Steve and Eydie
40	Brown-Eyed Handsome Man	Buddy Holly

Left **1964**: Priscilla White found fame as Cilla Black and the Italian song 'Il Mio Mondo' as 'You're My World'.

Below **1963**: The Beatles feared that Gerry and the Pacemakers might succeed in America before them, a notion that may seem odd in retrospect until one checks the table of 1963's top hits.

1964 TOP 40

No	Title	Artist
1	You're My World	Cilla Black
2	I Feel Fine	Beatles
3	Oh Pretty Woman	Roy Orbison
4	A Hard Day's Night	Beatles
5	Anyone Who Had A Heart	Cilla Black
6	Can't Buy Me Love	Beatles
7	(There's) Always Something There To Remind Me	Sandie Shaw
8	Needles And Pins	Searchers
9	It's Over	Roy Orbison
10	Glad All Over	Dave Clark Five
11	Have I The Right	Honeycombs
12	Little Children	Billy J. Kramer and the Dakotas
13	I'm Into Something Good	Herman's Hermits
14	Do Wah Diddy Diddy	Manfred Mann
15	Don't Throw Your Love Away	Searchers
16	I Want To Hold Your Hand	Beatles
17	A World Without Love	Peter and Gordon
18	You Really Got Me	Kinks
19	Baby Love	Supremes
20	It's All Over Now	Rolling Stones
21	Juliet	Four Pennies
22	Diane	Bachelors
23	House Of The Rising Sun	Animals
24	Little Red Rooster	Rolling Stones
25	Downtown	Petula Clark
26	Bits And Pieces	Dave Clark Five
27	I'm Gonna Be Strong	Gene Pitney
28	Someone Someone	Brian Poole and the Tremeloes
29	I'm The One	Gerry and the Pacemakers
30	Rag Doll	Four Seasons
31	All Day And All Of The Night	Kinks
32	I Believe	Bachelors
33	Hippy Hippy Shake	Swinging Blue Jeans
34	My Boy Lollipop	Millie
35	Just One Look	Hollies
36	I Won't Forget You	Jim Reeves
37	Where Did Our Love Go	Supremes
38	The Wedding	Julie Rogers
39	Call Up The Groups	Barron Knights
40	I Just Don't Know What To Do With Myself	Dusty Springfield

1965 TOP 40

No	Title	Artist
1	Tears	Ken Dodd
2	The Carnival Is Over	Seekers
3	Help	Beatles
4	Ticket To Ride	Beatles
5	I'm Alive	Hollies
6	The Last Time	Rolling Stones
7	Day Tripper/We Can Work It Out	Beatles
8	Get Off Of My Cloud	Rolling Stones
9	Long Live Love	Sandie Shaw
10	Crying In The Chapel	Elvis Presley
11	I Got You Babe	Sonny and Cher
12	I'll Never Find Another You	Seekers
13	(I Can't Get No) Satisfaction	Rolling Stones
14	Mr. Tambourine Man	Byrds
15	Yeh Yeh	Georgie Fame and the Blue Flames
16	You've Lost That Lovin' Feelin'	Righteous Brothers
17	It's Not Unusual	Tom Jones
18	Concrete And Clay	Unit Four Plus Two
19	Tired of Waiting For You	Kinks
20	Where Are You Now (My Love)	Jackie Trent
21	Make It Easy On Yourself	Walker Brothers
22	Go Now	Moody Blues
23	The Minute You're Gone	Cliff Richard
24	King Of The Road	Roger Miller
25	I Feel Fine	Beatles
26	Heart Full Of Soul	Yardbirds
27	Almost There	Andy Williams
28	Wind Me Up (Let Me Go)	Cliff Richard
29	My Generation	Who
30	You've Got Your Troubles	Fortunes
31	The Price Of Love	Everly Brothers
32	Here Comes The Night	Them
33	If You Gotta Go Go Now	Manfred Mann
34	True Love Ways	Peter and Gordon
35	We've Gotta Get Out Of This Place	Animals
36	Game Of Love	Wayne Fontana and the Mindbenders
37	You've Lost That Lovin' Feelin'	Cilla Black
38	A World Of Our Own	Seekers
39	Silhouettes	Herman's Hermits
40	Yesterday Man	Chris Andrews

1965: The engraving says it all: 'Tears' by Ken Dodd sold over one million copies in the UK.

1966 TOP 40

No	Title	Artist
1	**Distant Drums**	Jim Reeves
2	**Green Green Grass Of Home**	Tom Jones
3	**The Sun Ain't Gonna Shine Anymore**	Walker Brothers
4	**Yellow Submarine/Eleanor Rigby**	Beatles
5	**These Boots Are Made For Walkin'**	Nancy Sinatra
6	**Strangers In The Night**	Frank Sinatra
7	**Reach Out I'll Be There**	Four Tops
8	**Pretty Flamingo**	Manfred Mann
9	**Michelle**	Overlanders
10	**Good Vibrations**	Beach Boys
11	**Paperback Writer**	Beatles
12	**With A Girl Like You**	Troggs
13	**Sunny Afternoon**	Kinks
14	**Somebody Help Me**	Spencer Davis Group
15	**Day Tripper/We Can Work It Out**	Beatles
16	**Keep On Running**	Spencer Davis Group
17	**All Or Nothing**	Small Faces
18	**Out Of Time**	Chris Farlowe
19	**Paint It Black**	Rolling Stones
20	**You Don't Have To Say You Love Me**	Dusty Springfield
21	**Get Away**	Georgie Fame and the Blue Flames
22	**I Can't Let Go**	Hollies
23	**Nineteenth Nervous Breakdown**	Rolling Stones
24	**God Only Knows**	Beach Boys
25	**Bend It**	Dave Dee, Dozy, Beaky, Mick and Tich
26	**Daydream**	Lovin' Spoonful
27	**Morningtown Ride**	Seekers
28	**Stop Stop Stop**	Hollies
29	**What Would I Be**	Val Doonican
30	**I'm A Boy**	Who
31	**A Groovy Kind Of Love**	Mindbenders
32	**Wild Thing**	Troggs
33	**Black Is Black**	Los Bravos
34	**You Were On My Mind**	Crispian St. Peters
35	**Gimme Some Lovin'**	Spencer Davis Group
36	**I Can't Control Myself**	Troggs
37	**Semi-Detached Suburban Mr. James**	Manfred Mann
38	**Wind Me Up (Let Me Go)**	Cliff Richard
39	**Sloop John B.**	Beach Boys
40	**Nobody Needs Your Love**	Gene Pitney

1967 TOP 40

No	Title	Artist
1	**Release Me**...	Engelbert Humperdinck
2	**A Whiter Shade Of Pale**	Procol Harum
3	**The Last Waltz**................................	Engelbert Humperdinck
4	**Massachusetts**	Bee Gees
5	**San Francisco (Be Sure To Wear Some Flowers In Your Hair)**	Scott McKenzie
6	**I'm A Believer**.................................	Monkees
7	**Hello Goodbye**..................................	Beatles
8	**All You Need Is Love**	Beatles
9	**Puppet On A String**	Sandie Shaw
10	**Silence Is Golden**	Tremeloes
11	**Somethin' Stupid**.............................	Nancy Sinatra and Frank Sinatra
12	**Baby Now That I've Found You**.....	Foundations
13	**Let The Heartaches Begin**	Long John Baldry
14	**Green Green Grass Of Home**..........	Tom Jones
15	**This Is My Song**................................	Petula Clark
16	**I'll Never Fall In Love Again**	Tom Jones
17	**There Goes My Everything**	Engelbert Humperdinck
18	**Penny Lane/Strawberry Fields Forever**...	Beatles
19	**Waterloo Sunset**................................	Kinks
20	**Everybody Knows**............................	Dave Clark Five
21	**Flowers In The Rain**	Move
22	**Matthew And Son**.............................	Cat Stevens
23	**Excerpt From 'A Teenage Opera'**...	Keith West
24	**Morningtown Ride**	Seekers
25	**Dedicated To The One I Love**	Mamas and Papas
26	**Alternate Title**....................................	Monkees
27	**Hole In My Shoe**	Traffic
28	**It Must Be Him (Seul Sur Son Etoile)**..	Vikki Carr
29	**Edelweiss**..	Vince Hill
30	**Night Of Fear**.....................................	Move
31	**This Is My Song**................................	Harry Secombe
32	**I'm Coming Home**.............................	Tom Jones
33	**Sunshine Superman**...........................	Donovan
34	**Magical Mystery Tour (Double EP)**	Beatles
35	**A Little Bit Me, A Little Bit You**	Monkees
36	**Let's Spend The Night Together**.....	Rolling Stones
37	**Zabadak!**...	Dave Dee, Dozy, Beaky, Mick and Tich
38	**Death Of A Clown**	Dave Davies
39	**Carrie Anne**.......................................	Hollies
40	**If The Whole World Stopped Loving**	Val Doonican

Above **1968**: The Rolling Stones are shown in December 1968, the year of 'Jumping Jack Flash', only months before the death of Brian Jones (far left).

Above **1966**: Jim Reeves topped the British chart two years after his death and continued to have at least one country hit every year until 1984. Left **1967**: 'A Whiter Shade Of Pale' by Procol Harum was based on a Bach melody. The lyric was a poem by Keith Reid.

1968 TOP 40

No	Title	Artist
1	**Those Were The Days**	Mary Hopkin
2	**Young Girl**	Union Gap featuring Gary Puckett
3	**The Good, The Bad And The Ugly**	Hugo Montenegro
4	**What A Wonderful World/Cabaret**	Louis Armstrong
5	**Mony Mony**	Tommy James and the Shondells
6	**Cinderella Rockefella**	Esther and Abi Ofarim
7	**Lily the Pink**	Scaffold
8	**Baby Come Back**	Equals
9	**Hello Goodbye**	Beatles
10	**Hey Jude**	Beatles
11	**Everlasting Love**	Love Affair
12	**Mighty Quinn**	Manfred Mann
13	**Jumping Jack Flash**	Rolling Stones
14	**Congratulations**	Cliff Richard
15	**Lady Madonna**	Beatles
16	**I Gotta Get A Message To You**	Bee Gees
17	**Legend Of Xanadu**	Dave Dee, Dozy, Beaky, Mick and Tich
18	**Fire**	Crazy World of Arthur Brown
19	**Ballad Of Bonnie And Clyde**	Georgie Fame
20	**With A Little Help From My Friends**	Joe Cocker
21	**I Pretend**	Des O'Connor
22	**Do It Again**	Beach Boys
23	**A Man Without Love**	Engelbert Humperdinck
24	**Delilah**	Tom Jones
25	**Son Of Hickory Holler's Tramp**	O.C. Smith
26	**Eloise**	Barry Ryan
27	**Magical Mystery Tour (Double EP)**	Beatles
28	**Jesamine**	Casuals
29	**Honey**	Bobby Goldsboro
30	**Simon Says**	1910 Fruitgum Co.
31	**Ain't Got No – I Got Life/Do What You Gotta Do**	Nina Simone
32	**Lazy Sunday**	Small Faces
33	**Build Me Up Buttercup**	Foundations
34	**Little Arrows**	Leapy Lee
35	**This Guy's In Love With You**	Herb Alpert
36	**This Old Heart Of Mine**	Isley Brothers
37	**Am I That Easy To Forget**	Engelbert Humperdinck
38	**If I Only Had Time**	John Rowles
39	**Judy In Disguise (With Glasses)**	John Fred and the Playboy Band
40	**Bend Me Shape Me**	Amen Corner

1969 TOP 40

No	Title	Artist
1	Sugar Sugar	Archies
2	Get Back	Beatles with Billy Preston
3	Honky Tonk Woman	Rolling Stones
4	Where Do You Go To My Lovely	Peter Sarstedt
5	I Heard It Through The Grapevine	Marvin Gaye
6	Bad Moon Rising	Creedence Clearwater Revival
7	The Ballad Of John And Yoko	Beatles
8	In The Year 2525 (Exordium And Terminus)	Zager and Evans
9	Ob-La-Di Ob-La-Da	Marmalade
10	Something In The Air	Thunderclap Newman
11	(If Paradise Is) Half As Nice	Amen Corner
12	Two Little Boys	Rolf Harris
13	Albatross	Fleetwood Mac
14	I'll Never Fall In Love Again	Bobbie Gentry
15	Je T'Aime ... Moi Non Plus	Jane Birkin and Serge Gainsbourg
16	Dizzy	Tommy Roe
17	The Israelites	Desmond Dekker and the Aces
18	Blackberry Way	Move
19	Lily The Pink	Scaffold
20	Goodbye	Mary Hopkin
21	Ruby Don't Take Your Love To Town	Kenny Rogers and the First Edition
22	In The Ghetto	Elvis Presley
23	Give Peace A Chance	John Lennon/Plastic Ono Band
24	Saved By The Bell	Robin Gibb
25	Oh Well	Fleetwood Mac
26	(Call Me) Number One	Tremeloes
27	Oh Happy Day	Edwin Hawkins Singers
28	My Sentimental Friend	Herman's Hermits
29	Man Of The World	Fleetwood Mac
30	I'm Gonna Make You Mine	Lou Christie
31	Don't Forget To Remember	Bee Gees
32	Yester-Me Yester-You Yesterday	Stevie Wonder
33	Build Me Up Buttercup	Foundations
34	Gentle On My Mind	Dean Martin
35	Boom Bang-A-Bang	Lulu
36	For Once In My Life	Stevie Wonder
37	The Way It Used To Be	Engelbert Humperdinck
38	I'm Gonna Make You Love Me	Diana Ross and the Supremes and the Temptations
39	Please Don't Go	Donald Peers
40	He Ain't Heavy He's My Brother	Hollies

1969: 'I Heard It Through The Grapevine' had already been a million-seller for Gladys Knight and the Pips before Marvin Gaye made it what was then Tamla's biggest hit.

1970 TOP 40

No	Title	Artist
1	In The Summertime	Mungo Jerry
2	The Wonder Of You	Elvis Presley
3	Band Of Gold	Freda Payne
4	Love Grows (Where My Rosemary Goes)	Edison Lighthouse
5	I Hear You Knockin'	Dave Edmunds
6	Two Little Boys	Rolf Harris
7	Bridge Over Troubled Water	Simon and Garfunkel
8	Back Home	England World Cup Squad
9	Wand'rin' Star	Lee Marvin
10	Woodstock	Matthews Southern Comfort
11	Spirit In The Sky	Norman Greenbaum
12	All Kinds Of Everything	Dana
13	Tears Of A Clown	Smokey Robinson and the Miracles
14	Yellow River	Christie
15	Voodoo Chile	Jimi Hendrix Experience
16	All Right Now	Free
17	Patches	Clarence Carter
18	Ruby Don't Take Your Love To Town	Kenny Rogers and the First Edition
19	When I'm Dead And Gone	McGuinness Flint
20	Black Night	Deep Purple
21	Neanderthal Man	Hotlegs
22	You Can Get It If You Really Want	Desmond Dekker
23	Groovin' With Mr. Bloe	Mr. Bloe
24	Let's Work Together	Canned Heat
25	Lola	Kinks
26	Question	Moody Blues
27	Leavin' On A Jet Plane	Peter, Paul and Mary
28	Let It Be	Beatles
29	I Want You Back	Jackson Five
30	Knock Knock Who's There	Mary Hopkin
31	Suspicious Minds	Elvis Presley
32	Can't Help Falling In Love	Andy Williams
33	Cracklin' Rosie	Neil Diamond
34	Reflections Of My Life	Marmalade
35	Indian Reservation	Don Fardon
36	Give Me Just A Little More Time	Chairmen Of The Board
37	Mama Told Me Not To Come	Three Dog Night
38	Rainbow	Marmalade
39	All I Have To Do Is Dream	Bobbie Gentry and Glen Campbell
40	Up Around The Bend	Creedence Clearwater Revival

1970: Jimi Hendrix died on 18th September 1970 and had a posthumous number one within two months. On the original release, but not the charting re-issue, the artist credit was The Jimi Hendrix Experience.

Above **1972**: Long before Prince, Slade were the first act to distort the spellings of their song titles. Left **1971**: Rod Stewart simultaneously had the UK and US number one single ('Maggie May') and album (*Every Picture Tells A Story*).

1971 TOP 40

No	Title	Artist
1	Hot Love	T. Rex
2	Maggie May	Rod Stewart
3	Knock Three Times	Dawn
4	Chirpy Chirpy Cheep Cheep	Middle Of The Road
5	My Sweet Lord	George Harrison
6	I'm Still Waiting	Diana Ross
7	Coz I Luv You	Slade
8	Get It On	T. Rex
9	Hey Girl Don't Bother Me	Tams
10	Grandad	Clive Dunn
11	Ernie (The Fastest Milkman In The West)	Benny Hill
12	Double Barrel	Dave and Ansil Collins
13	Baby Jump	Mungo Jerry
14	I Hear You Knockin'	Dave Edmunds
15	Never Ending Song Of Love	New Seekers
16	Pushbike Song	Mixtures
17	Jeepster	T. Rex
18	Brown Sugar/Bitch/Let It Rock	Rolling Stones
19	Bridget The Midget	Ray Stevens
20	Witch Queen Of New Orleans	Redbone
21	Co-Co	Sweet
22	Another Day	Paul McCartney
23	I Did What I Did For Maria	Tony Christie
24	Did You Ever	Nancy and Lee
25	Indiana Wants Me	R. Dean Taylor
26	Tweedle Dee Tweedle Dum	Middle Of The Road
27	Don't Let It Die	Hurricane Smith
28	Ride A White Swan	T. Rex
29	Till	Tom Jones
30	Rose Garden	Lynn Anderson
31	When I'm Dead And Gone	McGuinness Flint
32	Banner Man	Blue Mink
33	Stoned Love	Supremes
34	Resurrection Shuffle	Ashton, Gardner and Dyke
35	What Are You Doing Sunday	Dawn
36	Simple Game	Four Tops
37	Johnny Reggae	Piglets
38	Heaven Must Have Sent You	Elgins
39	It Don't Come Easy	Ringo Starr
40	Devil's Answer	Atomic Rooster

1972 TOP 40

No	Title	Artist
1	Without You	Nilsson
2	Amazing Grace	The Pipes, Drums and Military Band of the Royal Scots Dragoon Guards
3	Puppy Love	Donny Osmond
4	My Ding-A-Ling	Chuck Berry
5	Mouldy Old Dough	Lieutenant Pigeon
6	I'd Like To Teach The World To Sing	New Seekers
7	Metal Guru	T. Rex
8	Son Of My Father	Chicory Tip
9	School's Out	Alice Cooper
10	Mama Weer All Crazee Now	Slade
11	Telegram Sam	T. Rex
12	Vincent	Don McLean
13	How Can I Be Sure	David Cassidy
14	Clair	Gilbert O'Sullivan
15	Long Haired Lover From Liverpool	Little Jimmy Osmond
16	You Wear It Well	Rod Stewart
17	Take Me Bak 'Ome	Slade
18	Ernie (The Fastest Milkman In The West)	Benny Hill
19	American Pie	Don McLean
20	Beg Steal Or Borrow	New Seekers
21	Mother Of Mine	Neil Reid
22	Crazy Horses	Osmonds
23	Rock 'n' Roll Parts 1 & 2	Gary Glitter
24	Children Of The Revolution	T. Rex
25	Donna	10 C.C.
26	Back Off Boogaloo	Ringo Starr
27	Seaside Shuffle	Terry Dactyl and the Dinosaurs
28	Sylvia's Mother	Dr. Hook and the Medicine Show
29	Could It Be Forever/Cherish	David Cassidy
30	Come What May	Vicky Leandros
31	Gudbuy T'Jane	Slade
32	Jeepster	T. Rex
33	Rocket Man	Elton John
34	Silver Machine	Hawkwind
35	Solid Gold Easy Action	T. Rex
36	You're A Lady	Peter Skellern
37	Alone Again (Naturally)	Gilbert O'Sullivan
38	A Horse With No Name	America
39	Breaking Up Is Hard To Do	Partridge Family
40	At The Club/Saturday Night At The Movies	Drifters

1973 TOP 40

No	Title	Artist
1	Blockbuster	Sweet
2	I Love You Love Me Love	Gary Glitter
3	Eye Level	Simon Park Orchestra
4	Tie A Yellow Ribbon Round The Old Oak Tree	Dawn
5	I'm The Leader Of The Gang (I Am)	Gary Glitter
6	Cum On Feel The Noize	Slade
7	See My Baby Jive	Wizzard
8	Young Love	Donny Osmond
9	Daydreamer/The Puppy Song	David Cassidy
10	Long Haired Lover From Liverpool	Little Jimmy Osmond
11	Skweeze Me Pleeze Me	Slade
12	Merry Xmas Everybody	Slade
13	Get Down	Gilbert O'Sullivan
14	Welcome Home	Peters and Lee
15	The Twelfth Of Never	Donny Osmond
16	Rubber Bullets	10 C.C.
17	Can The Can	Suzi Quatro
18	Angel Fingers	Wizzard
19	Hello Hello I'm Back Again	Gary Glitter
20	Part Of The Union	Strawbs
21	Ballroom Blitz	Sweet
22	Hell Raiser	Sweet
23	Let Me In	Osmonds
24	Do You Wanna Touch Me	Gary Glitter
25	Yesterday Once More	Carpenters
26	(Dancing) On A Saturday Night	Barry Blue
27	Jean Genie	David Bowie
28	My Frend Stan	Slade
29	Paper Roses	Marie Osmond
30	My Coo-Ca-Choo	Alvin Stardust
31	Albatross	Fleetwood Mac
32	Solid Gold Easy Action	T. Rex
33	Cindy Incidentally	Faces
34	Life On Mars	David Bowie
35	You Won't Find Another Fool Like Me	New Seekers
36	20th Century Boy	T. Rex
37	Sorrow	David Bowie
38	And I Love You So	Perry Como
39	Alright Alright Alright	Mungo Jerry
40	Rock On	David Essex

1974 TOP 40

No	Title	Artist
1	She	Charles Aznavour
2	Tiger Feet	Mud
3	Sugar Baby Love	Rubettes
4	Seasons In The Sun	Terry Jacks
5	Gonna Make You A Star	David Essex
6	Billy Don't Be A Hero	Paper Lace
7	Rock Your Baby	George McCrae
8	Everything I Own	Ken Boothe
9	Kung Fu Fighting	Carl Douglas
10	Love Me For A Reason	Osmonds
11	When Will I See You Again	Three Degrees
12	Devil Gate Drive	Suzi Quatro
13	Waterloo	Abba
14	You're The First The Last My Everything	Barry White
15	Merry Xmas Everybody	Slade
16	Lonely This Christmas	Mud
17	Annie's Song	John Denver
18	You Won't Find Another Fool Like Me	Seekers
19	Jealous Mind	Alvin Stardust
20	The Streak	Ray Stevens
21	Always Yours	Gary Glitter
22	Sad Sweet Dreamer	Sweet Sensation
23	Kissin' In The Back Row Of The Movies	Drifters
24	Teenage Rampage	Sweet
25	This Town Ain't Big Enough For The Both Of Us	Sparks
26	Killer Queen	Queen
27	You Ain't Seen Nothing Yet	Bachman-Turner Overdrive
28	Far Far Away	Slade
29	The Cat Crept In	Mud
30	The Air That I Breathe	Hollies
31	Hey Rock And Roll	Showaddywaddy
32	You Make Me Feel Brand New	Stylistics
33	The Show Must Go On	Leo Sayer
34	Born With A Smile On My Face	Stephanie De Sykes and Rain
35	I'm Leaving It (All) Up To You	Donny and Marie Osmond
36	The Most Beautiful Girl	Charlie Rich
37	Oh Yes! You're Beautiful	Gary Glitter
38	Shang-A-Lang	Bay City Rollers
39	Rock Me Gently	Andy Kim
40	Juke Box Jive	Rubettes

Above **1973**: Gary Glitter had two number ones and a pair of number twos in 1973. Left **1974**: Charles Aznavour is the only French solo artist to have topped the UK chart.

1975 TOP 40

No	Title	Artist
1	Bye Bye Baby	Bay City Rollers
2	Bohemian Rhapsody	Queen
3	Sailing	Rod Stewart
4	Whispering Grass	Windsor Davies and Don Estelle
5	Hold Me Close	David Essex
6	I Can't Give You Anything (But My Love)	Stylistics
7	Stand By Your Man	Tammy Wynette
8	Give A Little Love	Bay City Rollers
9	January	Pilot
10	I Only Have Eyes For You	Art Garfunkel
11	Space Oddity	David Bowie
12	If	Telly Savalas
13	I'm Not In Love	10 C.C.
14	Oh Boy	Mud
15	Make Me Smile (Come Up And See Me)	Steve Harley and Cockney Rebel
16	Lonely This Christmas	Mud
17	Barbados	Typically Tropical
18	Tears On My Pillow	Johnny Nash
19	D.I.V.O.R.C.E.	Billy Connolly
20	Ms Grace	Tymes
21	Down Down	Status Quo
22	You Sexy Thing	Hot Chocolate
23	There's A Whole Lot Of Loving	Guys and Dolls
24	Loving You	Minnie Riperton
25	Fox On The Run	Sweet
26	The Trail Of The Lonesome Pine	Laurel and Hardy with the Avalon Boys
27	The Streets Of London	Ralph McTell
28	The Last Farewell	Roger Whittaker
29	Three Steps To Heaven	Showaddywaddy
30	Please Mr. Postman	Carpenters
31	Misty	Ray Stevens
32	Love Is The Drug	Roxy Music
33	Moonlighting	Leo Sayer
34	Honey	Bobby Goldsboro
35	Never Can Say Goodbye	Gloria Gaynor
36	Goodbye My Love	Glitter Band
37	Wombling Merry Christmas	Wombles
38	There Goes My First Love	Drifters
39	The Bump	Kenny
40	The Hustle	Van McCoy

Above **1975**: Status Quo have had more top ten hits and weeks on chart than any British group except the Beatles, but they have only had a sole number one, 'Down Down'. Left **1976**: The Dutch act Pussycat were thrown in the deep end of the charts when their first hit was number one.

1976 TOP 40

No	Title	Artist
1	Save Your Kisses For Me	Brotherhood Of Man
2	Don't Go Breaking My Heart	Elton John and Kiki Dee
3	Dancing Queen	Abba
4	Fernando	Abba
5	Mississippi	Pussycat
6	Bohemian Rhapsody	Queen
7	If You Leave Me Now	Chicago
8	Under The Moon Of Love	Showaddywaddy
9	I Love To Love (But My Baby Loves To Dance)	Tina Charles
10	You To Me Are Everything	Real Thing
11	December '63 (Oh What A Night)	Four Seasons
12	Combine Harvester (Brand New Key)	Wurzels
13	Mamma Mia	Abba
14	Forever And Ever	Slik
15	No Charge	J.J. Barrie
16	When A Child Is Born (Soleado)	Johnny Mathis
17	The Roussos Phenomenon (EP)	Demis Roussos
18	A Little Bit More	Dr. Hook
19	Let 'Em In	Wings
20	Can't Get By Without You	Real Thing
21	When Forever Has Gone	Demis Roussos
22	You See The Trouble With Me	Barry White
23	Glass Of Champagne	Sailor
24	You Make Me Feel Like Dancing	Leo Sayer
25	Love Really Hurts Without You	Billy Ocean
26	Convoy	C. W. McCall
27	Silly Love Songs	Wings
28	Somebody To Love	Queen
29	Young Hearts Run Free	Candi Staton
30	The Trail Of The Lonesome Pine	Laurel and Hardy with the Avalon Boys
31	I Believe In Father Christmas	Greg Lake
32	You Just Might See Me Cry	Our Kid
33	The Killing Of Georgie	Rod Stewart
34	Jungle Rock	Hank Mizell
35	Jeans On	David Dundas
36	Music	John Miles
37	Sailing	Rod Stewart
38	Money Money Money	Abba
39	Love Machine	Miracles
40	Rodrigo's Guitar Concerto De Aranjuez	Manuel and his Music of the Mountains

1977 TOP 40

No	Title	Artist
1	**Knowing Me Knowing You**	Abba
2	**Way Down**	Elvis Presley
3	**Mull Of Kintyre/Girls' School**	Wings
4	**I Don't Want To Talk About It/**	
	First Cut Is The Deepest	Rod Stewart
5	**Don't Give Up On Us**	David Soul
6	**I Feel Love**	Donna Summer
7	**The Name Of The Game**	Abba
8	**Silver Lady**	David Soul
9	**So You Win Again**	Hot Chocolate
10	**When I Need You**	Leo Sayer
11	**Chanson D'Amour**	Manhattan Transfer
12	**Free**	Deniece Williams
13	**When A Child Is Born (Soleado)**	Johnny Mathis
14	**Don't Cry For Me Argentina**	Julie Covington
15	**Angelo**	Brotherhood Of Man
16	**Yes Sir I Can Boogie**	Baccara
17	**Lucille**	Kenny Rogers
18	**Show You The Way To Go**	Jacksons
19	**Float On**	Floaters
20	**The Floral Dance**	Brighouse and Rastrick Brass Band
21	**Black Is Black**	La Belle Epoque
22	**Magic Fly**	Space
23	**Going In With My Eyes Open**	David Soul
24	**We Are The Champions**	Queen
25	**Red Light Spells Danger**	Billy Ocean
26	**Under The Moon Of Love**	Showaddywaddy
27	**Fanfare For The Common Man**	Emerson, Lake and Palmer
28	**Ma Baker**	Boney M
29	**Ain't Gonna Bump No More**	
	(With No Big Fat Woman)	Joe Tex
30	**Boogie Nights**	Heatwave
31	**You Got What It Takes**	Showaddywaddy
32	**Sir Duke**	Stevie Wonder
33	**God Save The Queen**	Sex Pistols
34	**How Deep Is Your Love**	Bee Gees
35	**Side Show**	Barry Biggs
36	**Rockin' All Over The World**	Status Quo
37	**You're In My Heart**	Rod Stewart
38	**Money Money Money**	Abba
39	**Love Theme From *A Star Is**	
	Born (Evergreen)**	Barbra Streisand
40	**When**	Showaddywaddy

Left **1977**: The chart breakthrough of David Soul was a spin-off of his television success as Hutch in *Starsky and Hutch,* but he had actually begun his TV career as a vocalist wearing a ski mask under the pseudonym the Covered Man.

Right **1978**: Boney M had the most weeks on chart of any act in 1978.

Left **1979**: The Bee Gees waited over nine years between their second and third number ones, 'I've Gotta Get A Message To You' and 'Night Fever', but less than a year between the latter and their fourth list leader, 'Tragedy'.

1978 TOP 40

No	Title	Artist
1	**You're The One That I Want**	John Travolta and Olivia Newton-John
2	**Summer Nights**	John Travolta and Olivia Newton-John
3	**Rivers of Babylon/Brown Girl In The Ring**	Boney M
4	**Three Times A Lady**	Commodores
5	**Mull Of Kintyre/Girls' School**	Wings
6	**Wuthering Heights**	Kate Bush
7	**Mary's Boy Child/Oh My Lord**	Boney M
8	**Take A Chance On Me**	Abba
9	**Matchstalk Men and Matchstalk Cats And Dogs**	Brian and Michael
10	**Night Fever**	Bee Gees
11	**Rat Trap**	Boomtown Rats
12	**Figaro**	Brotherhood Of Man
13	**Uptown Top Ranking**	Althia and Donna
14	**Dreadlock Holiday**	10 C.C.
15	**Da Ya Think I'm Sexy**	Rod Stewart
16	**The Smurf Song**	Father Abraham and the Smurfs
17	**Denis**	Blondie
18	**Y.M.C.A.**	Village People
19	**Substitute**	Clout
20	**Rasputin**	Boney M
21	**Hopelessly Devoted To You**	Olivia Newton-John
22	**Love Don't Live Here Anymore**	Rose Royce
23	**The Floral Dance**	Brighouse and Rastrick Brass Band
24	**Boy From New York City**	Darts
25	**Come Back My Love**	Darts
26	**Sandy**	John Travolta
27	**It's Raining**	Darts
28	**I Wonder Why**	Showaddywaddy
29	**Love's Unkind**	Donna Summer
30	**Baker Street**	Gerry Rafferty
31	**Dancing In The City**	Marshall Hain
32	**A Taste Of Aggro**	Barron Knights
33	**Annie's Song**	James Galway
34	**Grease**	Frankie Valli
35	**Wishing On A Star**	Rose Royce
36	**Too Much Too Little Too Late**	Johnny Mathis and Deniece Williams
37	**If I Had Words**	Scott Fitzgerald and Yvonne Keeley
38	**Too Much Heaven**	Bee Gees
39	**Lucky Stars**	Dean Friedman
40	**Miss You**	Rolling Stones

1979 TOP 40

No	Title	Artist
1	Bright Eyes	Art Garfunkel
2	We Don't Talk Anymore	Cliff Richard
3	Are 'Friends' Electric	Tubeway Army
4	I Don't Like Mondays	Boomtown Rats
5	Heart Of Glass	Blondie
6	I Will Survive	Gloria Gaynor
7	When You're In Love With A Beautiful Woman	Dr. Hook
8	Y.M.C.A.	Village People
9	Sunday Girl	Blondie
10	One Day At A Time	Lena Martell
11	Message In A Bottle	Police
12	Another Brick In The Wall (Part II)	Pink Floyd
13	Ring My Bell	Anita Ward
14	Tragedy	Bee Gees
15	Hit Me With Your Rhythm Stick	Ian and the Blockheads
16	Cars	Gary Numan
17	Video Killed The Radio Star	Buggles
18	Walking On The Moon	Police
19	Dance Away	Roxy Music
20	Oliver's Army	Elvis Costello and the Attractions
21	Some Girls	Racey
22	Pop Muzik	M
23	Silly Games	Janet Kay
24	Crazy Little Thing Called Love	Queen
25	Chiquitita	Abba
26	In The Navy	Village People
27	I Have A Dream	Abba
28	Bang Bang	B.A. Robertson
29	Cool For Cats	Squeeze
30	Up The Junction	Squeeze
31	Dreaming	Blondie
32	Can't Stand Losing You	Police
33	Mary's Boy Child-Oh My Lord	Boney M
34	Woman In Love	Three Degrees
35	Lay Your Love On Me	Racey
36	Hooray Hooray It's A Holi-Holiday	Boney M
37	No More Tears (Enough Is Enough)	Donna Summer and Barbra Streisand
38	C'mon Everybody	Sex Pistols
39	Lucky Number	Lene Lovich
40	Don't Stop Till You Get Enough	Michael Jackson

1980 TOP 40

No	Title	Artist
1	**Don't Stand So Close To Me**	Police
2	**Woman In Love**	Barbra Streisand
3	**Crying**	Don McLean
4	**Super Trouper**	Abba
5	**Theme From M★A★S★H (Suicide Is Painless)**	Mash
6	**Going Underground/Dreams Of Children**	Jam
7	**Use It Up And Wear It Out**	Odyssey
8	**The Tide Is High**	Blondie
9	**Geno**	Dexy's Midnight Runners
10	**Coward Of The County**	Kenny Rogers
11	**Ashes To Ashes**	David Bowie
12	**Xanadu**	Olivia Newton-John and the Electric Light Orchestra
13	**Brass In Pocket**	Pretenders
14	**Atomic**	Blondie
15	**What's Another Year**	Johnny Logan
16	**The Winner Takes It All**	Abba
17	**Too Much Too Young (EP)**	Special AKA featuring Rico
18	**Working My Way Back To You – Forgive Me Girl**	Detroit Spinners
19	**Feels Like I'm In Love**	Kelly Marie
20	**Another Brick In The Wall (Part II)**	Pink Floyd
21	**Together We Are Beautiful**	Fern Kinney
22	**Start**	Jam
23	**There's No One Quite Like Grandma**	St. Winifred's School Choir
24	**Call Me**	Blondie
25	**(Just Like) Starting Over**	John Lennon
26	**D.I.S.C.O.**	Ottowan
27	**No Doubt About It**	Hot Chocolate
28	**Funky Town**	Lipps Inc.
29	**Dance Yourself Dizzy**	Liquid Gold
30	**Upside Down**	Diana Ross
31	**What You're Proposin'**	Status Quo
32	**One Day I'll Fly Away**	Randy Crawford
33	**With You I'm Born Again**	Billy Preston and Syreeta
34	**I Have A Dream**	Abba
35	**Coming Up**	Paul McCartney
36	**Masterblaster (Jammin')**	Stevie Wonder
37	**More Than I Can Say**	Leo Sayer
38	**And The Beat Goes On**	Whispers
39	**Take That Look Off Your Face**	Marti Webb
40	**Stop The Cavalry**	Jona Lewie

1981 TOP 40

No	Title	Artist
1	**Stand And Deliver**	Adam and the Ants
2	**Prince Charming**	Adam and the Ants
3	**Imagine**	John Lennon
4	**Green Door**	Shakin' Stevens
5	**It's My Party**	Dave Stewart with Barbara Gaskin
6	**This Ole House**	Shakin' Stevens
7	**Ghost Town**	Specials
8	**Making Your Mind Up**	Bucks Fizz
9	**Shaddup You Face**	Joe Dolce Music Theatre
10	**Don't You Want Me**	Human League
11	**Tainted Love**	Soft Cell
12	**One Day In Your Life**	Michael Jackson
13	**Woman**	John Lennon
14	**Being With You**	Smokey Robinson
15	**Under Pressure**	Queen and David Bowie
16	**Jealous Guy**	Roxy Music
17	**Begin The Beguine (Volver A Empezar)**	Julio Iglesias
18	**Japanese Boy**	Aneka
19	**Every Little Thing She Does Is Magic**	Police
20	**There's No One Quite Like Grandma**	St. Winifred's School Choir
21	**Vienna**	Ultravox
22	**You Drive Me Crazy**	Shakin' Stevens
23	**Happy Birthday**	Altered Images
24	**Daddy's Home**	Cliff Richard
25	**Hooked On Classics**	Royal Philharmonic Orchestra, Conductor Louis Clark
26	**Chi Mai** (Theme From The TV Series *The Life And Times Of David Lloyd George)*	Ennio Morricone
27	**Kids In America**	Kim Wilde
28	**Birdie Song (Birdie Dance)**	Tweets
29	**Antmusic**	Adam and the Ants
30	**Stars On 45 Vol. 2**	Starsound
31	**Stars On 45**	Starsound
32	**More Than In Love**	Kate Robbins and Beyond
33	**In The Air Tonight**	Phil Collins
34	**Happy Birthday**	Stevie Wonder
35	**Happy Xmas (War Is Over)**	John Lennon
36	**Invisible Sun**	Police
37	**O Superman**	Laurie Anderson
38	**Kings Of The Wild Frontier**	Adam and the Ants
39	**(Just Like) Starting Over**	John Lennon
40	**Can Can**	Bad Manners

Above **1980**: In the only case of a number one sequel to a number one original, 'Ashes To Ashes' by David Bowie continued the saga of Major Tom from 'Space Oddity'. **1981**: The only single issued in 1981 to sell a million copies in Britain was 'Don't You Want Me' by the Human League, which sold in seven figures in America as well.

1982 TOP 40

No	Title	Artist
1	**Come On Eileen**	Dexys Midnight Runners
2	**Eye Of The Tiger**	Survivor
3	**Fame**	Irene Cara
4	**The Lion Sleeps Tonight**	Tight Fit
5	**Do You Really Want To Hurt Me**	Culture Club
6	**Ebony And Ivory**	Paul McCartney with Stevie Wonder
7	**I Don't Wanna Dance**	Eddy Grant
8	**Seven Tears**	Goombay Dance Band
9	**Pass The Dutchie**	Musical Youth
10	**Town Called Malice/Precious**	Jam
11	**Goody Two Shoes**	Adam Ant
12	**The Land Of Make Believe**	Bucks Fizz
13	**House Of Fun**	Madness
14	**Don't You Want Me**	Human League
15	**Beat Surrender**	Jam
16	**Save Your Love**	Renée and Renato
17	**Happy Talk**	Captain Sensible
18	**A Little Peace**	Nicole
19	**My Camera Never Lies**	Bucks Fizz
20	**Oh Julie**	Shakin' Stevens
21	**The Model/Computer Love**	Kraftwerk
22	**I've Never Been To Me**	Charlene
23	**Mirror Man**	Human League
24	**Golden Brown**	Stranglers
25	**Abracadabra**	Steve Miller Band
26	**Heartbreaker**	Dionne Warwick
27	**Mickey**	Toni Basil
28	**The Bitterest Pill (I Ever Had To Swallow)**	Jam
29	**Torch**	Soft Cell
30	**Zoom**	Fat Larry's Band
31	**Save A Prayer**	Duran Duran
32	**Only You**	Yazoo
33	**Just An Illusion**	Imagination
34	**Private Investigations**	Dire Straits
35	**Ain't No Pleasing You**	Chas and Dave
36	**This Time (We'll Get It Right)/England We'll Fly The Flag**	England World Cup Squad
37	**The Shakin' Stevens EP**	Shakin' Stevens
38	**Da Da Da**	Trio
39	**One Step Further**	Bardo
40	**Annie, I'm Not Your Daddy**	Kid Creole and the Coconuts

1983 TOP 40

No	Title	Artist
1	**Karma Chameleon**	Culture Club
2	**Uptown Girl**	Billy Joel
3	**Every Breath You Take**	Police
4	**True**	Spandau Ballet
5	**Only You**	Flying Pickets
6	**Red Red Wine**	UB40
7	**Wherever I Lay My Hat (That's My Home)**	Paul Young
8	**Down Under**	Men At Work
9	**Baby Jane**	Rod Stewart
10	**Give It Up**	K.C. and the Sunshine Band
11	**Let's Dance**	David Bowie
12	**You Can't Hurry Love**	Phil Collins
13	**Total Eclipse Of The Heart**	Bonnie Tyler
14	**Too Shy**	Kajagoogoo
15	**Is There Something I Should Know**	Duran Duran
16	**Save Your Love**	Renée and Renato
17	**Billie Jean**	Michael Jackson
18	**Candy Girl**	New Edition
19	**I.O.U.**	Freeez
20	**Love Of The Common People**	Paul Young
21	**All Night Long (All Night)**	Lionel Richie
22	**Say Say Say**	Paul McCartney and Michael Jackson
23	**Bad Boys**	Wham!
24	**They Don't Know**	Tracey Ullman
25	**My Oh My**	Slade
26	**Gold**	Spandau Ballet
27	**Words**	F.R. David
28	**Church Of The Poison Mind**	Culture Club
29	**Electric Avenue**	Eddy Grant
30	**Sweet Dreams (Are Made Of This)**	Eurythmics
31	**Flashdance ... What A Feeling**	Irene Cara
32	**Keep Feeling Fascination**	Human League
33	**Tonight I Celebrate My Love**	Peabo Bryson and Roberta Flack
34	**Modern Love**	David Bowie
35	**Temptation**	Heaven 17
36	**A Winter's Tale**	David Essex
37	**China Girl**	David Bowie
38	**Wings Of A Dove**	Madness
39	**The Shakin' Stevens EP**	Shakin' Stevens
40	**Beat It**	Michael Jackson

Left **1982**: The only number one by Madness, 'House Of Fun', was the biggest of their 15 top ten hits.

1984: 'Hello' by Lionel Richie (below) and 'I Just Called To Say I Love You' by Stevie Wonder, the longest-running Motown number ones, appeared in the same year.

Left **1983**: The Police captured Britain's number one of 1980 with 'Don't Stand So Close To Me' and America's number one of 1983 with 'Every Breath You Take'.

1984 TOP 40

No	Title	Artist
1	Two Tribes	Frankie Goes To Hollywood
2	I Just Called To Say I Love You	Stevie Wonder
3	Hello	Lionel Richie
4	Relax!	Frankie Goes To Hollywood
5	The Reflex	Duran Duran
6	Careless Whisper	George Michael
7	I Feel For You	Chaka Khan
8	99 Red Balloons	Nena
9	Freedom	Wham!
10	Do They Know It's Christmas	Band Aid
11	Wake Me Up Before You Go-Go	Wham!
12	Pipes Of Peace	Paul McCartney
13	I Should Have Known Better	Jim Diamond
14	The Power Of Love	Frankie Goes To Hollywood
15	Only You	Flying Pickets
16	Ghostbusters	Ray Parker Jr.
17	Against All Odds (Take A Look At Me Now)	Phil Collins
18	Hole In My Shoe	neil
19	Last Christmas/Everything She Wants	Wham!
20	Agadoo	Black Lace
21	Joanna/Tonight	Kool And The Gang
22	A Love Worth Waiting For	Shakin' Stevens
23	Let's Hear It For The Boy	Deniece Williams
24	Automatic	Pointer Sisters
25	Radio Ga Ga	Queen
26	Wild Boys	Duran Duran
27	The War Song	Culture Club
28	No More Lonely Nights	Paul McCartney
29	I Won't Let The Sun Go Down On Me	Nik Kershaw
30	You Take Me Up	Thompson Twins
31	Girls Just Want To Have Fun	Cyndi Lauper
32	What Is Love	Howard Jones
33	It's Raining Men	Weather Girls
34	My Oh My	Slade
35	I Want To Break Free	Queen
36	That's Living Alright	Joe Fagin
37	We All Stand Together	Paul McCartney and The Frog Chorus
38	Doctor Doctor	Thompson Twins
39	Street Dance	Break Machine
40	Robert De Niro's Waiting	Bananarama

1985 TOP 40

No	Title	Artist
1	The Power Of Love	Jennifer Rush
2	19	Paul Hardcastle
3	I Know Him So Well	Elaine Paige and Barbara Dickson
4	Frankie	Sister Sledge
5	Easy Lover	Philip Bailey (duet with Phil Collins)
6	Into The Groove	Madonna
7	Dancing In The Street	David Bowie and Mick Jagger
8	I Want To Know What Love Is	Foreigner
9	I'm Your Man	Wham!
10	Saving All My Love For You	Whitney Houston
11	Do They Know It's Christmas	Band Aid
12	A Good Heart	Feargal Sharkey
13	You Spin Me Round (Like A Record)	Dead or Alive
14	We Are The World	USA For Africa
15	You'll Never Walk Alone	Crowd
16	I Got You Babe	UB40 (guest vocals Chrissie Hynde)
17	Move Closer	Phyllis Nelson
18	There Must Be An Angel (Playing With My Heart)	Eurythmics
19	If I Was	Midge Ure
20	Merry Christmas Everyone	Shakin' Stevens
21	Axel F	Harold Faltermeyer
22	Love And Pride	King
23	Take On Me	a-ha
24	A View To A Kill	Duran Duran
25	Holding Out For A Hero	Bonnie Tyler
26	Everybody Wants To Rule The World	Tears For Fears
27	Last Christmas/Everything She Wants	Wham!
28	That Ole Devil Called Love	Alison Moyet
29	Welcome To The Pleasuredome	Frankie Goes To Hollywood
30	Crazy For You	Madonna
31	Kayleigh	Marillion
32	1999/Little Red Corvette	Prince and the Revolution
33	Holiday	Madonna
34	Trapped	Colonel Abrams
35	Solid	Ashford and Simpson
36	See The Day	Dee C. Lee
37	We Don't Need Another Hero (Thunderdome)	Tina Turner
38	Pie Jesu	Sarah Brightman and Paul Miles-Kingston
39	Part-Time Lover	Stevie Wonder
40	I Feel Love (Medley)	Bronski Beat and Marc Almond

1986 TOP 40

No	Title	Artist
1	**Don't Leave Me This Way**	Communards with Sarah Jane Morris
2	**When The Going Gets Tough, The Tough Get Going**	Billy Ocean
3	**Take My Breath Away (Love Theme From *Top Gun*)**	Berlin
4	**Papa Don't Preach**	Madonna
5	**The Lady In Red**	Chris De Burgh
6	**Chain Reaction**	Diana Ross
7	**I Want To Wake Up With You**	Boris Gardiner
8	**Living Doll**	Cliff Richard and the Young Ones featuring Hank B. Marvin
9	**A Different Corner**	George Michael
10	**Every Loser Wins**	Nick Berry
11	**Spirit In The Sky**	Doctor and the Medics
12	**The Chicken Song**	Spitting Image
13	**The Sun Always Shines On T.V.**	a-ha
14	**The Edge Of Heaven/Where Did Your Heart Go**	Wham!
15	**The Final Countdown**	Europe
16	**West End Girls**	Pet Shop Boys
17	**Rock Me Amadeus**	Falco
18	**True Blue**	Madonna
19	**Caravan Of Love**	Housemartins
20	**Reet Petite**	Jackie Wilson
21	**Merry Christmas Everyone**	Shakin' Stevens
22	**On My Own**	Patti Labelle and Michael McDonald
23	**So Macho/Cruising**	Sinitta
24	**We Don't Have To**	Jermaine Stewart
25	**Rain Or Shine**	Five Star
26	**You Keep Me Hangin' On**	Kim Wilde
27	**Holding Back The Years**	Simply Red
28	**Saving All My Love For You**	Whitney Houston
29	**I Can't Wait**	Nu Shooz
30	**In The Army Now**	Status Quo
31	**Walk Of Life**	Dire Straits
32	**Borderline**	Madonna
33	**Manic Monday**	Bangles
34	**Every Beat Of My Heart**	Rod Stewart
35	**Sometimes**	Erasure
36	**Wonderful World**	Sam Cooke
37	**Starting Together**	Su Pollard
38	**Absolute Beginners**	David Bowie
39	**Live To Tell**	Madonna
40	**Only Love**	Nana Mouskouri

1987 TOP 40

No	Title	Artist
1	Never Gonna Give You Up	Rick Astley
2	China In Your Hand	T'Pau
3	Nothing's Gonna Stop Us Now	Starship
4	You Win Again	Bee Gees
5	It's A Sin	Pet Shop Boys
6	Reet Petite	Jackie Wilson
7	Stand By Me	Ben E. King
8	Let It Be	Ferry Aid
9	I Wanna Dance With Somebody (Who Loves Me)	Whitney Houston
10	Pump Up The Volume/Anitina (The First Time I See She Dance)	M/A/R/R/S
11	I Knew You Were Waiting (For Me)	George Michael and Aretha Franklin
12	La Isla Bonita	Madonna
13	Jack Your Body	Steve 'Silk' Hurley
14	Star Trekkin'	Firm
15	La Bamba	Los Lobos
16	Everything I Own	Boy George
17	I Just Can't Stop Loving You	Michael Jackson
18	Always On My Mind	Pet Shop Boys
19	Respectable	Mel and Kim
20	Who's That Girl	Madonna
21	Can't Be With You Tonight	Judy Boucher
22	Got My Mind Set On You	George Harrison
23	Under The Boardwalk	Bruce Willis
24	Full Metal Jacket (I Wanna Be Your Drill Instructor)	Abigail Mead and Nigel Goulding
25	What Have I Done To Deserve This	Pet Shop Boys and Dusty Springfield
26	Heartache	Pepsi and Shirley
27	When I Fall In Love/My Arms Keep Missing You	Rick Astley
28	When A Man Loves A Woman	Percy Sledge
29	Faith	George Michael
30	Caravan Of Love	Housemartins
31	Hold Me Now	Johnny Logan
32	Wipeout	Fat Boys and Beach Boys
33	A Boy From Nowhere	Tom Jones
34	Call Me	Spagna
35	Crockett's Theme	Jan Hammer
36	Fairytale of New York	Pogues and Kirsty MacColl
37	Is This Love	Alison Moyet
38	Whenever You Need Somebody	Rick Astley
39	Down To Earth	Curiosity Killed The Cat
40	I Get The Sweetest Feeling	Jackie Wilson

Top **1985**: The Communards (Richard Coles and Jimmy Somerville) topped the chart with Sarah Jane Morris on a remake of a Harold Melvin and the Bluenotes hit. Right **1986**: Madonna was the artist with the most weeks on chart for three consecutive years (1985-87), a record for consistent achievement. She is shown on the set of the 'Papa Don't Preach' video. Below **1987**: The Pet Shop Boys (Chris Lowe and Neil Tennant) amassed the most weeks at number one in 1987.

1988 TOP 40

No	Title	Artist
1	I Should Be So Lucky	Kylie Minogue
2	The Only Way Is Up	Yazz and the Plastic Population
3	With A Little Help From My Friends/She's Leaving Home	Wet Wet Wet/Billy Bragg with Cara Tivey
4	Nothing's Gonna Change My Love For You	Glenn Medeiros
5	Mistletoe And Wine	Cliff Richard
6	I Think We're Alone Now	Tiffany
7	Heart	Pet Shop Boys
8	The First Time	Robin Beck
9	Orinoco Flow	Enya
10	Heaven Is A Place On Earth	Belinda Carlisle
11	He Ain't Heavy He's My Brother	Hollies
12	Groovy Kind Of Love	Phil Collins
13	Theme From S Express	S Express
14	I Owe You Nothing	Bros
15	Always On My Mind	Pet Shop Boys
16	One Moment In Time	Whitney Houston
17	Don't Turn Around	Aswad
18	Perfect	Fairground Attraction
19	Desire	U2
20	Doctorin' The Tardis	Timelords
21	The Loco-motion	Kylie Minogue
22	Drop The Boy	Bros
23	Especially For You	Kylie Minogue & Jason Donovan
24	Push It/Tramp	Salt-N-Pepa
25	Je Ne Sais Pas Pourquoi	Kylie Minogue
26	Got To Be Certain	Kylie Minogue
27	The Twist (Yo, Twist)	Fat Boys with Chubby Checker
28	The Harder I Try	Brother Beyond
29	Beat Dis	Bomb The Bass
30	Together Forever	Rick Astley
31	Stand Up For Your Love Rights	Yazz
32	Sign Your Name	Terence Trent D'Arby
33	When Will I Be Famous	Bros
34	Don't Worry Be Happy	Bobby McFerrin
35	Love Changes (Everything)	Climie Fisher
36	Cat Among The Pigeons/Silent Night	Bros
37	Need You Tonight	INXS
38	Fairytale Of New York	Pogues/Kirsty MacColl
39	Teardrops	Womack & Womack
40	Get Outta My Dreams Get Into My Car	Billy Ocean

Below **1989**: Within the first half of this year Jason Donovan had two solo number ones and a chart-topping duet with his soap opera co-star Kylie Minogue.

Above **1988**: Kylie Minogue began her chart career with six top two hits, an unequalled start.

1989 TOP 40

No	Title	Artist
1	Ride On Time	Black Box
2	Swing The Mood	Jive Bunny & The Mastermixers
3	Eternal Flame	Bangles
4	Back To Life (However Do You Want Me)	Soul II Soul featuring Caron Wheeler
5	Something's Gotten Hold Of My Heart	Marc Almond featuring Gene Pitney
6	Like A Prayer	Madonna
7	That's What I Like	Jive Bunny & The Mastermixers
8	You Got It (The Right Stuff)	New Kids On The Block
9	Especially For You	Kylie Minogue & Jason Donovan
10	Ferry 'Cross The Mersey	Christians, Gerry Marsden, Paul McCartney, Holly Johnson & Stock Aitken Waterman
11	Too Many Broken Hearts	Jason Donovan
12	All Around The World	Lisa Stansfield
13	You'll Never Stop Me Loving You	Sonia
14	Sealed With A Kiss	Jason Donovan
15	Belfast Child	Simple Minds
16	Do They Know It's Christmas	Band Aid II
17	Hand On Your Heart	Kylie Minogue
18	Let's Party	Jive Bunny & the Mastermixers
19	Girl I'm Gonna Miss You	Milli Vanilli
20	If You Don't Know Me By Now	Simply Red
21	The Living Years	Mike & The Mechanics
22	Crackers International EP	Erasure
23	Love Changes Everything	Michael Ball
24	Pump Up The Jam	Technotronic featuring Felly
25	Right Here Waiting	Richard Marx
26	Don't Know Much	Linda Ronstadt with Aaron Neville
27	Wouldn't Change A Thing	Kylie Minogue
28	The Best Of Me	Cliff Richard
29	Miss You Like Crazy	Natalie Cole
30	London Nights	London Boys
31	When You Come Back To Me	Jason Donovan
32	French Kiss	Lil' Louis
33	Song For Whoever	Beautiful South
34	Batdance	Prince
35	Every Day (I Love You More)	Jason Donovan
36	Poison	Alice Cooper
37	Another Day In Paradise	Phil Collins
38	Leave Me Alone	Michael Jackson
39	Too Much	Bros
40	This Time I Know It's For Real	Donna Summer

1990 TOP 40

No	Title	Artist
1	**Sacrifice/Healing Hands**	Elton John
2	**Nothing Compares 2 U**	Sinead O'Connor
3	**Unchained Melody**	Righteous Brothers
4	**Dub Be Good To Me**	Beats International
5	**Ice Ice Baby**	Vanilla Ice
6	**Killer**	Adamski
7	**Show Me Heaven**	Maria McKee
8	**Turtle Power**	Partners In Kryme
9	**Vogue**	Madonna
10	**Itsy Bitsy Teeny Weeny Yellow Polka Dot Bikini**	Bombalurina
11	**World In Motion**	Englandneworder
12	**The Power**	Snap
13	**The Joker**	Steve Miller Band
14	**Hangin' Tough**	New Kids On The Block
15	**Do They Know It's Christmas**	Band Aid II
16	**Tears On My Pillow**	Kylie Minogue
17	**A Little Time**	Beautiful South
18	**Saviour's Day**	Cliff Richard
19	**Nessun Dorma**	Luciano Pavarotti
20	**Tom's Diner**	DNA featuring Suzanne Vega
21	**Love Shack**	B52's
22	**Get Up (Before The Night Is Over)**	Technotronic featuring Ya Kid K
23	**Black Velvet**	Alannah Myles
24	**Groove Is In The Heart/What Is Love**	Deee-Lite
25	**Better The Devil You Know**	Kylie Minogue
26	**Four Bacharach And David Songs EP**	Deacon Blue
27	**The Brits 1990**	Various Artists
28	**When You Come Back To Me**	Jason Donovan
29	**Dirty Cash**	Adventures Of Stevie V
30	**Mona**	Craig McLachlan and Check 1-2
31	**Opposites Attract**	Paula Abdul with the Wild Pair
32	**Blue Velvet**	Bobby Vinton
33	**Don't Worry**	Kim Appleby
34	**I've Been Thinking About You**	Londonbeat
35	**Justify My Love**	Madonna
36	**Anniversary Waltz–Part 1**	Status Quo
37	**Hanky Panky**	Madonna
38	**Fog On The Tyne (Revisited)**	Gazza and Lindisfarne
39	**Step By Step**	New Kids On The Block
40	**How Am I Supposed To Live Without You**	Michael Bolton

1991 TOP 40

No	Title	Artist
1	(Everything I Do) I Do It For You	Bryan Adams
2	The Shoop Shoop Song (It's In His Kiss)	Cher
3	The One And Only	Chesney Hawkes
4	I Wanna Sex You Up	Color Me Badd
5	Do The Bartman	Simpsons
6	Any Dream Will Do	Jason Donovan
7	3am Eternal	KLF
8	Dizzy	Vic Reeves & The Wonderstuff
9	Don't Let The Sun Go Down On Me	George Michael & Elton John
10	Black Or White	Michael Jackson
11	Should I Stay Or Should I Go	Clash
12	Bring Your Daughter ... To The Slaughter	Iron Maiden
13	Bohemian Rhapsody/These Are The Days Of Our Lives	Queen
14	The Stonk	Hale & Pace and the Stonkers
15	Sadness Part 1	Enigma
16	The Fly	U2
17	Innuendo	Queen
18	I'm Too Sexy	Right Said Fred
19	Sit Down	James
20	Get Ready For This	2 Unlimited
21	More Than Words	Extreme
22	Let's Talk About Sex	Salt-N-Pepa
23	Last Train To Trancentral	KLF
24	Wind Of Change	Scorpions
25	When You Tell Me That You Love Me	Diana Ross
26	Crazy For You	Madonna
27	(I Wanna Give You) Devotion	Nomad featuring MC Mikee Freedom
28	Baby Baby	Amy Grant
29	Gypsy Woman (La Da Dee)	Crystal Waters
30	Now That We Found Love	Heavy D & The Boyz
31	Crazy	Seal
32	Ice Ice Baby	Vanilla Ice
33	Insanity	Oceanic
34	Rhythm Of My Heart	Rod Stewart
35	Chorus	Erasure
36	Justified & Ancient	KLF featuring Tammy Wynette
37	Charly	Prodigy
38	Set Adrift On Memory Bliss	PM Dawn
39	You Could Be Mine	Guns N' Roses
40	Promise Me	Beverley Craven

Above **1990**: 'Unchained Melody' gave the Righteous Brothers the longest gap between number one hits, 25 years 259 days. Top **1991**: Over a quarter of a century elapsed between the first solo hit and first solo number one for Cher. Right **1992**: 'End Of The Road' by Boyz II Men surpassed Elvis Presley's rock era record of 11 weeks atop the American Billboard Hot 100 with 'Don't Be Cruel'/'Hound Dog', only to be overtaken within weeks by Whitney Houston's 'I Will Always Love You'.

1992 TOP 40

No	Title	Artist
1	Stay	Shakespears Sister
2	Rhythm Is A Dancer	Snap
3	Please Don't Go	KWS
4	Abba-Esque EP	Erasure
5	Ebeneezer Goode	Shamen
6	Goodnight Girl	Wet Wet Wet
7	Bohemian Rhapsody	Queen
8	I Will Always Love You	Whitney Houston
9	End Of The Road	Boyz II Men
10	Deeply Dippy	Right Said Fred
11	Ain't No Doubt	Jimmy Nail
12	Would I Lie To You	Charles & Eddie
13	Sleeping Satellite	Tasmin Archer
14	On A Ragga Tip	SL2
15	Heal The World	Michael Jackson
16	It's My Life	Dr. Alban
17	Barcelona	Freddie Mercury & Montserrat Caballe
18	My Girl	Temptations
19	I Love Your Smile	Shanice
20	The Best Things In Life Are Free	Luther Vandross and Janet Jackson
21	Heartbeat	Nick Berry
22	Justified And Ancient	KLF featuring Tammy Wynette
23	I'll Be There	Mariah Carey
24	Baker Street	Undercover
25	Sesame Street	Smart E's
26	People Everyday	Arrested Development
27	Twilight Zone	2 Unlimited
28	Jump	Kris Kross
29	Knockin' On Heaven's Door	Guns N' Roses
30	Give Me Just A Little More Time	Kylie Minogue
31	Everybody In The Place (EP)	Prodigy
32	Finally	Ce Ce Peniston
33	Let's Get Rocked	Def Leppard
34	Be Quick Or Be Dead	Iron Maiden
35	Raving I'm Raving	Shut Up And Dance
36	To Be With You	Mr Big
37	Hazard	Richard Marx
38	Achy Breaky Heart	Billy Ray Cyrus
39	This Used To Be My Playground	Madonna
40	I'm Gonna Get You	Bizarre Inc featuring Angie Brown

PART THREE

THE

ARTISTS

AN ALPHABETICAL LISTING OF THE ARTISTS WHO MADE THE TOP 1000 HITS

1993: George Michael appears at the 1992 Freddie Mercury Tribute Concert at Wembley, where he performed 'Somebody To Love' with Queen.

---------- **A** ----------

ABBA
46	Dancing Queen	Epic EPC 4499
69	Knowing Me Knowing You	Epic EPC 4955
111	Fernando	Epic EPC 4036
203	The Name Of The Game	Epic EPC 5750
235	Take A Chance On Me	Epic EPC 5950
311	Super Trouper	Epic EPC 9089
437	Waterloo	Epic EPC 2240
447	Mamma Mia	Epic EPC 3790
489	The Winner Takes It All	Epic EPC 8835
682	I Have A Dream	Epic EPC 8088
853	Chiquitita	Epic EPC 7030

ADAM AND THE ANTS
105	Stand And Deliver	CBS A 1065
167	Prince Charming	CBS A 1408
384	Goody Two Shoes	CBS A 2367
892	Antmusic	CBS 9352

Goody Two Shoes *credited to Adam Ant*

BRYAN ADAMS
1	(Everything I Do) I Do It For You	A&M AM 789

ADAMSKI
160	Killer	MCA MCA 1400

ADVENTURES OF STEVIE V
974	Dirty Cash	Mercury MER 311

A-HA
428	The Sun Always Shines On T.V.	Warner Bros. W 8846
728	Take On Me	Warner Bros. W 9006

ALICE COOPER
300	School's Out	Warner Bros. K 16188

ALLISONS
652	Are You Sure	Fontana H 294

MARC ALMOND FEATURING GENE PITNEY
200	Something's Gotten Hold Of My Heart	Parlophone R 6201

See also Gene Pitney

ALTERED IMAGES
771	Happy Birthday	Epic EPCA 1522

ALTHIA AND DONNA
579	Up Town Top Ranking	Lightning LIG 506

AMEN CORNER
440	(If Paradise Is) Half As Nice	Immediate IM 073

ANEKA
622	Japanese Boy	Hansa HANSA 5

ANIMALS
638	House Of The Rising Sun	Columbia D7301

PAUL ANKA
6	Diana	Columbia DB 39980

TASMIN ARCHER
451	Sleeping Satellite	EMI EM 233

ARCHIES
12	Sugar Sugar	RCA 1872

LOUIS ARMSTRONG
148	What A Wonderful World/Cabaret	HMV POP 1615

RICK ASTLEY
79	Never Gonna Give You Up	RCA PB 41447
915	When I Fall In Love/My Arms Keep Missing You	RCA PB 41683
919	Together Forever	RCA PB 41817

ASWAD
516	Don't Turn Around	Mango IS 341

WINIFRED ATWELL
216	Poor People Of Paris	Decca F 10681

CHARLES AZNAVOUR
172	She	Barclay BAR 26

---------- **B** ----------

BACCARA
551	Yes Sir I Can Boogie	RCA PB 5526

BACHELORS
603	Diane	Decca F 11799
935	I Believe	Decca F 11857

BACHMAN-TURNER OVERDRIVE
856	You Ain't Seen Nothin' Yet	Mercury 6167025

PHILIP BAILEY WITH PHIL COLLINS
159	Easy Lover	CBS A 4915

LONG JOHN BALDRY
472	Let The Heartaches Begin	Pye 7N 17385

MICHAEL BALL
818	Love Changes Everything	Really UsefulRUR 3

BAND AID
74	Do They Know It's Christmas	Mercury FEED 1

BAND AID II
363	Do They Know It's Christmas	PWL/Polydor FEED 2

BANGLES
169	Eternal Flame	CBS BANGS 5

J.J. BARRIE
571	No Charge	Power Exchange PX 209

TONI BASIL
872	Mickey	Radialchoice TIC 4

SHIRLEY BASSEY
117	As I Love You	Philips PB 845
552	Reach For The Stars/Climb Ev'ry Mountain	Columbia DB 4685
661	As Long As He Needs Me	Columbia DB 4490

BAY CITY ROLLERS
44	Bye Bye Baby	Bell 1409
321	Give A Little Love	Bell 1425

BEACH BOYS
427	Good Vibrations	Capitol CL 15475
618	Do It Again	Capitol CL 15554
804	God Only Knows	Capitol CL 15459

BEATLES
18	From Me To You	Parlophone R 5015
24	Hello Goodbye	Parlophone R 5655
25	She Loves You	Parlophone R 5055

BRIAN AND MICHAEL
276 Matchstalk Men and Matchstalk Cats and Dogs
....Pye 7N 46035

BRIGHOUSE AND RASTRICK BRASS BAND
656 The Floral Dance...............Transatlantic BIG 548

BROS
486 I Owe You Nothing.....................CBS ATOM 4
683 Drop The Boy..............................CBS ATOM 3

BROTHER BEYOND
864 The Harder I Try..................Parlophone R 6184

BROTHERHOOD OF MAN
37 Save Your Kisses For Me ....Pye 7N 45569
530 Angelo..............................Pye 7N 45699
563 Figaro ....Pye 7N 46037

CRAZY WORLD OF ARTHUR BROWN
576 Fire.....................................Track 604022

JOE BROWN AND THE BRUVVERS
783 A Picture Of You..................Piccadilly 7N 35047

BUCKS FIZZ
312 Making Your Mind Up........................RCA 56
417 The Land Of Make Believe....................RCA 163
597 My Camera Never Lies.......................RCA 202

BUGGLES
594 Video Killed The Radio Star......Island WIP 6524

B. BUMBLE AND THE STINGERS
548 Nut Rocker..........................Top Rank JAR 611

LOU BUSCH
668 Zambesi....................................Capitol CL 14504

KATE BUSH
195 Wuthering Heights...............................EMI 2719

BYRDS
457 Mr. Tambourine Man......................CBS 201765

———————— **C** ————————

CANNED HEAT
960 Let's Work Together................Liberty LBF 15302

CAPTAIN SENSIBLE
519 Happy Talk.....................................A&M CAP 1

IRENE CARA
241 Fame...RSO 90

MARIAH CAREY
926 I'll Be There..........................Columbia 6581377

BELINDA CARLISLE
403 Heaven Is A Place On Earth.........Virgin VS 1036

CARPENTERS
889 Yesterday Once More.................A&M AMS 7073

CLARENCE CARTER
724 Patches......................................Atlantic 2091030

DAVID CASSIDY
303 Daydreamer/The Puppy Song...............Bell 1334
461 How Can I Be Sure...............................Bell 1258
994 Could It Be Forever/Cherish.................Bell 1224

CASUALS
938 Jesamine...Decca F 22784

CHARLENE
629 I've Never Been To Me........Motown TMG 1260

RAY CHARLES
389 I Can't Stop Loving You............HMV POP 1034

TINA CHARLES
279 I Love To Love (But My Baby Loves To
Dance) ....CBS 3937

CHARLES AND EDDIE
387 Would I Lie To You.....................Capitol CL 673

CHUBBY CHECKER
785 Let's Twist Again....................Columbia DB 4691
See also Fat Boys with Chubby Checker

CHER
65 The Shoop Shoop Song (It's In His Kiss)
....Epic 6566737
See also Sonny and Cher

CHICAGO
240 If You Leave Me Now..........................CBS 4603

CHICORY TIP
291 Son Of My Father...............................CBS 7737

CHRISTIANS, GERRY MARSDEN, PAUL McCARTNEY, HOLLY JOHNSON AND STOCK AITKEN WATERMAN
360 Ferry Cross The Mersey.................PWL PWL 41

CHRISTIE
549 Yellow River....................................CBS 4911

LOU CHRISTIE
962 I'm Gonna Make You Mine........Buddah 201057

TONY CHRISTIE
875 I Did What I Did For Maria........MCA MK 5064

PETULA CLARK
507 This Is My Song ....Pye 7N 17258
531 Sailor ....Pye 7N 15324
743 Downtown ....Pye 7N 15722

DAVE CLARK FIVE
378 Glad All Over.......................Columbia DB 7154
756 Bits And Pieces.....................Columbia DB 7210
821 Everybody Knows..................Columbia DB 8286

CLASH
498 Should I Stay Or Should I Go
....Columbia 6566677

CLOUT
801 Substitute................................Carrere EMI 2788

EDDIE COCHRAN
390 Three Steps To Heaven ....London HLG 9115

JOE COCKER
596 With A Little Help From My Friends
................................Regal-Zonophone RZ 3013

NAT 'KING' COLE
932 When I Fall In Love.................Capitol CL 14709

NATALIE COLE
977 Miss You Like Crazy...............EMI-USA MT 63

DAVE AND ANSIL COLLINS
453 Double Barrel........................Technique TE 901

PHIL COLLINS
406 You Can't Hurry Love ....Virgin VS 531
430 A Groovy Kind Of Love ....Virgin VS 1117
723 Against All Odds (Take A Look At Me Now)
....Virgin VS 674
See also Philip Bailey with Phil Collins

COLOR ME BADD
258 I Wanna Sex You Up ....Giant W 0036

COMMODORES
91 Three Times A Lady ....Motown TMG 1113

COMMUNARDS AND SARAH JANE MORRIS
152 Don't Leave Me This Way ....London LON 103

PERRY COMO
8 Magic Moments.................................RCA 1036

BILLY CONNOLLY
630 D.I.V.O.R.C.E. ....Polydor 2058 652

RUSS CONWAY
140 Side Saddle ....Columbia DB 4256
414 Roulette ....Columbia DB 4298

ELVIS COSTELLO AND THE ATTRACTIONS
715 Oliver's Army...............................Radar ADA 31

JULIE COVINGTON
527 Don't Cry For Me Argentina................MCA 260

FLOYD CRAMER
649 On The Rebound.............................RCA 1231

RANDY CRAWFORD
907 One Day I'll Fly Away ....Warner Bros. K 17680

CREEDENCE CLEARWATER REVIVAL
250 Bad Moon Rising..................Liberty LBF 15230

CRICKETS
278 That'll Be The Day............Vogue-Coral Q 72279

CROWD
515 You'll Never Walk Alone ....Spartan BRAD 1

CRYSTALS
832 Then He Kissed Me ....London HLU 9773

CULTURE CLUB
48 Karma Chameleon........................Virgin VS 612
288 Do You Really Want To Hurt Me
....Virgin VS 518
923 Church Of The Poison Mind.........Virgin VS 571

---------------- **D** ----------------

TERRY DACTYL AND THE DINOSAURS
901 Seaside Shuffle..UK 5

JIM DALE
927 Be My Girl ....Parlophone R 4343

VIC DAMONE
392 On The Street Where You Live .....Philips PB 819

DANA
404 All Kinds Of Everything ....Rex R 11054

BOBBY DARIN
107 Dream Lover..........................London HLE 8867
369 Mack The Knife ....London HLE 8939
972 Things....................................London HLK 9575

DARTS
950 Boy From New York City ....Magnet MAG 116
969 Come Back My Love..............Magnet MAG 110
971 It's Raining ....Magnet MAG 126

F.R. DAVID
899 Words ....Carrere CAR 248

WINDSOR DAVIES AND DON ESTELLE
233 Whispering Grass ....EMI 2290

SPENCER DAVIS GROUP
479 Somebody Help Me ....Fontana TF 679
542 Keep On Running ....Fontana TF 632

DAWN
63 Knock Three Times ....Bell 1146
143 Tie A Yellow Ribbon Round
The Old Oak Tree ....Bell 1287

DORIS DAY
26 Whatever Will Be Will Be.............Philips PB 586

CHRIS DE BURGH
251 The Lady In Red ....A&M AM 331

DEACON BLUE
909 Four Bacharach And David Songs EP
....CBS DEAC 12

DEAD OR ALIVE
493 You Spin Me Round (Like A Record)
....Epic A 4861

JIMMY DEAN
944 Big Bad John ....Philips PB 1187

DAVE DEE, DOZY, BEAKY, MICK AND TICH
570 Legend Of Xanadu ....Fontana TF 903
874 Bend It.......................................Fontana TF 746

DEEE-LITE
846 Groove Is In The Heart/What Is Love
....Elektra EKR 114

DEEP PURPLE
806 Black Night ....Harvest HAR 5020

DESMOND DEKKER AND THE ACES
607 Israelites.............................Pyramid PYR 6058
845 You Can Get It If You Really Want
....Trojan TR 7777
You Can Get It If You Really Want *credited to Desmond Dekker*

JOHN DENVER
565 Annie's Song...........................RCA APBO 0295

DETROIT SPINNERS
511 Working My Way Back To You-
Forgive Me Girl........................Atlantic K 11432

DEXY'S MIDNIGHT RUNNERS
126 Come On Eileen ....Mercury DEXYS 9
431 Geno........................Late Night Feelings R 6033

JIM DIAMOND
578 I Should Have Known Better ....A&M AM 220

DNA FEATURING SUZANNE VEGA
736 Tom's Diner ....A&M AM 592

DOCTOR AND THE MEDICS
350 Spirit In The Sky ....IRS IRM 113

DR. ALBAN
752   It's My Life ....Arista 115330

DR. HOOK
242   When You're In Love With A Beautiful
       Woman ....Capitol CL 16039
657   A Little Bit More ....Capitol CL 15871
981   Sylvia's Mother....................................CBS 7929
       Sylvia's Mother *credited to Dr. Hook's Medicine Show*

KEN DODD
59   Tears......................................Columbia DB 7659

JOE DOLCE MUSIC THEATRE
347   Shaddup You Face........................Epic EPC 9518

LONNIE DONEGAN
101   Cumberland Gap ....Pye Nixa B 15087
171   My Old Man's A Dustman ....Pye 7N 15256
368   Gamblin' Man/Putting On The Style
       .... Pye Nixa N 15093
691   Lost John/Stewball ....Pye Nixa N 15036
780   Battle Of New Orleans ....Pye 7N 15026

JASON DONOVAN
377   Any Dream Will Do...........Really Useful RUR 7
385   Too Many Broken Hearts...............PWL PWL 32
497   Sealed With A Kiss ....PWL PWL 39
705   When You Come Back To Me ......PWL PWL 46
       See also Kylie Minogue and Jason Donovan

VAL DOONICAN
947   What Would I Be.........................Decca F 12505

CARL DOUGLAS
309   Kung Fu Fighting ....Pye 7N 45377

CRAIG DOUGLAS
113   Only Sixteen..........................Top Rank JAR 159

DREAMWEAVERS
223   It's Almost Tomorrow................Brunswick 05515

DRIFTERS
666   Save The Last Dance For Me ..London HLK 9201
757   Kissin' In The Back Row Of The Movies
       ....Bell 1358

JOHNNY DUNCAN AND THE BLUEGRASS BOYS
786   Last Train To San Fernando ...Columbia DB 3959

CLIVE DUNN
253   Grandad..................................Columbia DB 8726

DURAN DURAN
190   The Reflex ....EMI DURAN 2
483   Is There Something I Should Know .....EMI 5371
775   A View To A Kill........Parlophone DURAN 007

— **E** —

DUANE EDDY
967   Because They're Young..........London HLW 9162

EDISON LIGHTHOUSE
102   Love Grows (Where My Rosemary Goes)
       ....Bell 1091

DAVE EDMUNDS
39   I Hear You Knockin' ....MAM 1

TOMMY EDWARDS
281   It's All In The Game............................MGM 989

ELIAS AND HIS ZIG ZAG JIVE FLUTES
675   Tom Hark.............................Columbia DB 4109

EMERSON LAKE AND PALMER
942   Fanfare For The Common Man .Atlantic K 10946

ENGLAND WORLD CUP SQUAD
238   Back Home ....Pye 7N 17920
       See also Englandneworder

ENGLANDNEWORDER
423   World In Motion... ....Factory/MCA FAC 2937
       See also England World Cup Squad; New Order

ENIGMA
616   Sadness Part 1 ....Virgin Int. DINS 101

ENYA
365   Orinoco Flow ....WEA YZ 312

EQUALS
345   Baby Come Back.......................President PT 135

ERASURE
103   Abba-esque EP ....Mute MUTE 114
696   Crackers International EP...........Mute MUTE 93

DAVID ESSEX
246   Gonna Make You A Star ....CBS 2492
267   Hold Me Close ....CBS 3572

EUROPE
441   The Final Countdown ....Epic A 7127

EURYTHMICS
577   There Must Be An Angel (Playing With
       My Heart) ....RCA PB 40247

EVERLY BROTHERS
14   All I Have To Do Is Dream/Claudette
       ....London HLA 8618
20   Cathy's Clown ....Warner Bros. WB 1
274   Walk Right Back/Ebony Eyes
       ....Warner Bros. WB 33
509   Temptation ....Warner Bros. WB 42
789   Wake Up Little Susie ....London HLA 8498
951   Bird Dog ....London HLA 8685
990   The Price Of Love............Warner Bros. WB 161

EXTREME
839   More Than Words........................A&M AM 792

— **F** —

FAIRGROUND ATTRACTION
556   Perfect...RCA PB 41845

ADAM FAITH
222   What Do You Want ....Parlophone R 4591
615   Poor Me ....Parlophone R 4623
954   Someone Else's Baby ....Parlophone R 4643

FALCO
561   Rock Me Amadeus ....A&M AM 278

HAROLD FALTERMEYER
714   Axel F ....MCA MCA 949

GEORGIE FAME AND THE BLUE FLAMES
491   Yeh Yeh ....Columbia DB 7428

586	Ballad Of Bonnie and Clyde	CBS 3124
650	Get Away	Columbia DB 7946

Ballad of Bonnie and Clyde *credits only Georgie Fame*

CHRIS FARLOWE
582 Out Of Time ....Immediate IM 035

FAT BOYS WITH CHUBBY CHECKER
838 The Twist (Yo, Twist).................Urban URB 20
See also Chubby Checker

FAT LARRY'S BAND
999 Zoom.......................................WMOT VS 546

FATHER ABRAHAM AND THE SMURFS
654 The Smurf Song...........................Decca F 13759

FERRY AID
361 Let It Be ....The Sun AID 1

FIRM
480 Star Trekkin' ....Bark TREK 1

FIVE STAR
843 Rain Or Shine ....Tent PB 40901

FLEETWOOD MAC
525 Albatross...........................Blue Horizon 573145
824 Oh Well ....Reprise RS 27000
948 Man Of The World.................Immediate IM 080

FLOATERS
617 Float On..ABC 4187

FLYING PICKETS
106 Only You ....10 TEN 14

EMILE FORD AND THE CHECKMATES
28 What Do You want To Make Those Eyes At Me For ....Pye 7N 15525

TENNESSEE ERNIE FORD
133 Sixteen Tons...........................Capitol CL 14500

FOREIGNER
349 I Want To Know What Love Is
....Atlantic A 9596

FORTUNES
961 You've Got Your Troubles.............Decca F 12173

FOUNDATIONS
416 Baby Now That I've Found You ....Pye 7N 17366
787 Build Me Up Buttercup ....Pye 7N 17638

FOUR ACES
779 Love Is A Many Splendored Thing
....Brunswick 05480

FOUR PENNIES
566 Juliet...Philips BF 1322

FOUR PREPS
829 Big Man.................................Capitol CL 14873

FOUR SEASONS
409 December '63 (Oh What A Night)
....Warner Bros. K 16688
902 Rag Doll ....Philips BF 1347

FOUR TOPS
287 Reach Out I'll Be There
....................................Tamla Motown TMG 579

CONNIE FRANCIS
31 Who's Sorry Now ....MGM 975
35 Carolina Moon/Stupid Cupid ....MGM 985
968 Mama/Robot Man..........................MGM 1076

FRANKIE GOES TO HOLLYWOOD
7 Two Tribes ....ZTT ZTAS 3
53 Relax!..ZTT ZTAS 1
644 The Power Of Love ....ZTT ZTAS 5
920 Welcome To The Pleasuredome......ZTT ZTAS 7

ARETHA FRANKLIN AND GEORGE MICHAEL
433 I Knew You Were Waiting (For Me) .Epic DUET 2
See also George Michael

FREDDIE AND THE DREAMERS
857 I'm Telling You Now.............Columbia DB 7068

FREE
660 All Right Now..........................Island WIP 6082

FREEEZ
700 I.O.U. ....Beggars Banquet BEG 96

G

BORIS GARDINER
260 I Want To Wake Up With You...Revue REV 733

ART GARFUNKEL
49 Bright Eyes...CBS 6947
398 I Only Have Eyes For You...................CBS 2575
See also Simon and Garfunkel

MARVIN GAYE
243 I Heard It Through The Grapevine
......................................Tamla Motown TMG 686

GLORIA GAYNOR
189 I Will Survive ....Polydor 2095017

BOBBIE GENTRY
538 I'll Never Fall In Love Again ....Capitol CL 15606

GERRY AND THE PACEMAKERS
131 You'll Never Walk Alone ....Columbia DB 7126
135 I Like It ....Columbia DB 7041
232 How Do You Do It ....Columbia DB 4987
894 I'm The One ....Columbia DB 7189

ROBIN GIBB
791 Saved By The Bell ....Polydor 56377

GARY GLITTER
110 I Love You Love Me Love ....Bell 1337
155 I'm The Leader Of The Gang (I Am) ....Bell 1321
627 Always Yours...Bell 1359
713 Hello Hello I'm Back Again ....Bell 1299
729 Rock And Roll (Parts 1 & 2).................Bell 1216
807 Do You Wanna Touch Me (Oh Yeah)....Bell 1280

BOBBY GOLDSBORO
782 Honey ....United Artists UP 2215

GOOMBAY DANCE BAND
324 Seven Tears...............................Epic EPC A 1242

EDDY GRANT
323 I Don't Wanna Dance..........................Ice ICE 56

NORMAN GREENBAUM
381 Spirit In The Sky....................Reprise RS 20885

GUYS AND DOLLS
836 There's A Whole Lot Of Loving.....Magnet MAG 20

H

HALE AND PACE AND THE STONKERS
598 The Stonk ....London LON 296

BILL HALEY AND HIS COMETS
54 Rock Around The Clock..........Brunswick 05317

RUSS HAMILTON
978 We Will Make Love ....Oriole CB 1359

PAUL HARDCASTLE
97 19..Chrysalis CHS 2860

STEVE HARLEY AND COCKNEY REBEL
478 Make Me Smile (Come Up And See Me)
....EMI 2263

JET HARRIS AND TONY MEEHAN
348 Diamonds ....Decca F 11563
976 Scarlett O'Hara ....Decca F 11644

ROLF HARRIS
33 Two Little Boys......................Columbia DB 8630

GEORGE HARRISON
83 My Sweet Lord ....Apple R 5884
681 Got My Mind Set On You ...Dark Horse W 8178

CHESNEY HAWKES
90 The One And Only.............Chrysalis CHS 3627

EDWIN HAWKINS SINGERS
867 Oh Happy Day ....Buddah 201048

BILL HAYES
731 Ballad Of Davy Crockett ....London HLA 8220

HEATWAVE
988 Boogie Nights..................................GTO GT 77

JIMI HENDRIX EXPERIENCE
591 Voodoo Chile ....Track 2095 001

HERMAN'S HERMITS
401 I'm Into Something Good .....Columbia DB 7338
904 My Sentimental Friend ....Columbia DB 8563

HIGHWAYMEN
613 Michael ....HMV POP 910

BENNY HILL
118 Ernie (The Fastest Milkman In The West)
....Columbia DB 8833

RONNIE HILTON
50 No Other Love...........................HMV POP 198

MICHAEL HOLLIDAY
367 The Story Of My Life ....Columbia DB 4058
643 Starry Eyed ....Columbia DB 4378

HOLLIES
307 I'm Alive................................Parlophone R 5287
393 He Ain't Heavy He's My Brother ......EMI EM 74
739 I Can't Let Go ....Parlophone R 5409
913 Stop Stop Stop ....Parlophone R 5508
949 The Air That I Breathe ....Polydor 2058 435

BUDDY HOLLY
211 It Doesn't Matter Anymore..........Coral Q 72360

HONEYCOMBS
391 Have I The Right ....Pye 7N 15664

MARY HOPKIN
38 Those Were The Days............................Apple 2
730 Goodbye ....Apple 10

HOT CHOCOLATE
283 So You Win Again ....RAK 259
710 You Sexy Thing.....................................RAK 221
751 No Doubt About It ....RAK 310

HOTLEGS
812 Neanderthal Man ....Fontana 6007019

HOUSEMARTINS
533 Caravan Of Love ....Go! Discs GOD 16

WHITNEY HOUSTON
3 I Will Always Love You ....Arista 74321120657
373 Saving All My Love For You ....Arista ARIST 640
382 I Wanna Dance With Somebody (Who Loves
Me) ....Arista RIS 1
513 One Moment In Time...................Arista 111613

HUMAN LEAGUE
92 Don't You Want Me ....Virgin VS 466
777 Mirror Man ....Virgin VS 522

ENGELBERT HUMPERDINCK
36 Release Me...................................Decca F 12541
71 The Last Waltz ....Decca F 12655
677 There Goes My Everything..........Decca F 12610
711 A Man Without Love...................Decca F 12770

TAB HUNTER
13 Young Love....................................London HLD 8380

STEVE 'SILK' HURLEY
477 Jack Your Body ....DJ International LON 117

I

IAN AND THE BLOCKHEADS
536 Hit Me With Your Rhythm Stick ....Stiff BUY 38

FRANK IFIELD
15 I Remember You...................Columbia DB 4856
72 Lovesick Blues ....Columbia DB 4913
319 Wayward Wind.....................Columbia DB 4960
370 Confessin' ....Columbia DB 7062

JULIO IGLESIAS
610 Begin The Beguine (Volver
A Empezar) ....CBS A 1612

IRON MAIDEN
523 Bring Your Daughter...To The
Slaughter...................................EMI EMPD 171

J

TERRY JACKS
187 Seasons In The Sun ....Bell 1344

MICHAEL JACKSON
405 One Day In Your Life ....Motown TMG 976
490 Black Or White ....Epic 6575987
518 I Just Can't Stop Loving You ....Epic 6502027
569 Billie Jean ....Epic EPC A 3084

LIPPS INC.
792   Funky Town........................Casablanca CAN 194

LIQUID GOLD
831   Dance Yourself Dizzy................................Polo 1

LITTLE EVA
725   The Loco-Motion....................London HL 9581

LOS LOBOS
494   La Bamba.....................................Slash LASH 13

JOHNNY LOGAN
481   What's Another Year ....Epic EPC 8572
992   Hold Me Now................................Epic LOG 1

LONDON BOYS
997   London Nights.............................WEA YZ 393

LOVE AFFAIR
397   Everlasting Love ....CBS 3125

LOVIN' SPOONFUL
881   Daydream................................Pye Int 7N 25361

———————— M ————————

M
790   Pop Muzik ....MCA 413

C.W. McCALL
996   Convoy..MGM 2006560

PAUL McCARTNEY
5   Mull Of Kintyre/Girls School ......Capitol R 6018
503   Pipes Of Peace ....Parlophone R 6064
766   Let 'Em In ....Parlophone R 6015
822   Another Day ....Apple R 5889
    Mull Of Kintyre and Let 'Em In credited to Wings;
    See also Paul McCartney with Stevie Wonder, Paul
    McCartney and Michael Jackson; Christians, Gerry
    Marsden, Paul McCartney, Holly Johnson and Stock
    Aitken Waterman

PAUL McCARTNEY AND MICHAEL JACKSON
819   Say Say Say ....Parlophone R 6062
    See also Paul McCartney; Michael Jackson

PAUL McCARTNEY WITH STEVIE WONDER
305   Ebony And Ivory ....Parlophone R 6054
    See also Paul McCartney; Stevie Wonder

GEORGE McCRAE
284   Rock Your Baby ....Jayboy BOY 85

McGUINNESS FLINT
685   When I'm Dead And Gone ......Capitol CL 15662

MARIA McKEE
163   Show Me Heaven ....Epic 6563037

SCOTT McKENZIE
141   San Francisco (Be Sure To Wear Some Flowers
    In Your Hair) ....CBS 2816

CRAIG McLACHLAN AND CHECK 1-2
995   Mona..Epic 6557847

DON McLEAN
308   Crying ....EMI 5051
426   Vincent.........................United Artists UP 35359
697   American Pie ....United Artists UP 35325

RALPH McTELL
891   Streets Of London ....Reprise K 14380

MADNESS
496   House Of Fun...............................Stiff BUY 146

MADONNA
162   Into The Groove.........................Sire W 8934
202   Vogue ....Sire W 9851
248   Papa Don't Preach ....Sire W 8836
304   Like A Prayer...................................Sire W 7539
445   La Isla Bonita ....Sire W 8378
572   True Blue ....Sire W 8550
581   Who's That Girl..............................Sire W 8341
687   Crazy For You ....Geffen A 6323

MAMAS AND THE PAPAS
956   Dedicated To The One I Love ....RCA 1576

MANFRED MANN
327   Pretty Flamingo ....HMV POP 1523
408   Mighty Quinn...........................Fontana TF 897
419   Do Wah Diddy Diddy ....HMV POP 1320

MANHATTAN TRANSFER
343   Chanson D'Amour ....Atlantic K 10886

MARCELS
468   Blue Moon..............................Pye Int 7N 25073

KELLY MARIE
514   Feels Like I'm In Love ....Calibre PLUS 1

MARINO MARINI
753   Come Prima ....Durium DC 16632

MARMALADE
351   Ob-La-Di Ob-La-Da ....CBS 3892

M/A/R/R/S
407   Pump Up The Volume/Anitina (The First Time I
    See She Dance) ....4AD AD 707

LENA MARTELL
330   One Day At A Time ....Pye 7N 46021

DEAN MARTIN
183   Memories Are Made Of This
    ....Capitol CL 14523
695   Volare..Capitol CL 14910
933   Return To Me ....Capitol CL 14844

TONY MARTIN
940   Walk Hand In Hand ....HMV POP 222

LEE MARVIN
254   Wand'rin' Star.................Paramount PARA 3004

RICHARD MARX
873   Right Here Waiting ....EMI-USA MT 72

MASH
316   Theme From M*A*S*H* (Suicide Is Painless)
    ....CBS 8536

JOHNNY MATHIS
269   When A Child Is Born (Soleado) ....CBS 4599

MATTHEWS SOUTHERN COMFORT
326   Woodstock.....................................Uni UNS 526

ABIGAIL MEAD AND NIGEL GOULDING
883   Full Metal Jacket (I Wanna Be Your Drill
    Instructor) ....Warner Bros. W 8187

GLENN MEDEIROS
198   Nothing's Gonna Change My Love For You
    ....London LON 184

MEL AND KIM
541   Respectable ....Supreme SUPE 111

MEN AT WORK
266   Down Under............................Epic EPC A 1980

FREDDIE MERCURY AND MONTSERRAT CABALLE
767   Barcelona ....Polydor PO 211

GEORGE MICHAEL
228   Careless Whisper...............................Epic A 4603
315   A Different Corner ....Epic A 7033
924   Faith ....Epic EMU 3
       See also Aretha Franklin and George Michael;
       George Michael and Elton John; George Michael
       and Queen

GEORGE MICHAEL AND ELTON JOHN
459   Don't Let The Sun Go Down On Me
       ....Epic 6576467
       See also George Michael; Elton John

GEORGE MICHAEL AND QUEEN
317   Five Live EP ....Parlophone R 6340
       See also George Michael; Queen

MIDDLE OF THE ROAD
64   Chirpy Chirpy Cheep Cheep..............RCA 2047
966   Tweedle Dee Tweedle Dum ....RCA 2110

MIKE AND THE MECHANICS
748   The Living Years ....WEA U 7717

NED MILLER
688   From A Jack To A King.............London HL 9648

ROGER MILLER
632   King Of The Road.....................Philips BF 1397

STEVE MILLER BAND
499   The Joker.....................................Capitol CL 583
847   Abracadabra ....Mercury STEVE 3

MILLI VANILLI
733   Girl I'm Gonna Miss You .....Cooltempo COOL 191

MILLIE
952   My Boy Lollipop ....Fontana TF 449

MINDBENDERS
987   A Groovy Kind Of Love..............Fontana TF 644
       See also Wayne Fontana and the Mindbenders

KYLIE MINOGUE
85   I Should Be So Lucky.....................PWL PWL 8
540   Hand On Your Heart....................PWL PWL 35
583   Tears On My Pillow......................PWL PWL 47
676   The Loco-Motion ....PWL PWL 14
741   Je Ne Sais Pas Pourquoi ....PWL PWL 21
761   Got To Be Certain ....PWL PWL 12
858   Better The Devil You Know..........PWL PWL 56
880   Wouldn't Change A Thing............PWL PWL 42
       See also Kylie Minogue and Jason Donovan

KYLIE MINOGUE AND JASON DONOVAN
220   Especially For You ....PWL PWL 42
       See also Kylie Minogue; Jason Donovan

MR. BLOE
945   Groovin' With Mr. Bloe ....DJM DJLS 216

GUY MITCHELL
215   Singing The Blues ....Philips PB 650
550   Rock-A-Billy ....Philips PB 685

MIXTURES
667   Pushbike Song ....Polydor 2058 053

MONKEES
149   I'm A Believer ....RCA 1580
979   Alternate Title ....RCA 1604

HUGO MONTENEGRO
146   The Good, The Bad And The Ugly....RCA 1727

CHRIS MONTEZ
678   Let's Dance ....London HLU 9596

MOODY BLUES
606   Go Now ....Decca F 12022
991   Question....................................Threshold TH 4

JANE MORGAN
633   The Day The Rains Came .....London HLR 8751

ENNIO MORRICONE
833   Chi Mai (Theme From *The Life and Times of
       David Lloyd George*) ....BBC RESL 92

MOVE
626   Blackberry Way........Regal Zonophone RZ 3015
830   Flowers In The Rain .....Regal Zonophone RZ 3001

ALISON MOYET
912   That Ole Devil Called Love.............CBS A 6044

MUD
175   Tiger Feet..RAK 166
205   Lonely This Christmas ....RAK 187
474   Oh Boy ....RAK 201
886   The Cat Crept In ....RAK 170

MUNGO JERRY
23   In The Summertime ....Dawn DNX 2502
487   Baby Jump ....Dawn DNX 2505

MUSICAL YOUTH
333   Pass The Dutchie..........................MCA YOU 1

ALANNAH MYLES
817   Black Velvet ....East West A 8742

--------------- **N** ---------------

JIMMY NAIL
293   Ain't No Doubt......................East West YZ 686

NANCY AND LEE
953   Did You Ever.............................Reprise K 14093
       See also Nancy Sinatra

JOHNNY NASH
553   Tears On My Pillow ....CBS 3220

neil
769   Hole In My Shoe ....WEA YZ 10

PHYLLIS NELSON
560   Move Closer.....................................Carrere 337

RICKY NELSON
823   Hello Mary Lou/Travellin' Man
       ....London HLP 9347

NENA
270 99 Red Balloons ....Epic A 4074

NEW EDITION
646 Candy Girl ....London LON 21

NEW KIDS ON THE BLOCK
354 You Got It (The Right Stuff) ....CBS BLOCK 2
502 Hangin' Tough ....CBS BLOCK 3

NEW SEEKERS
161 I'd Like To Teach The World To Sing
....Polydor 2058 184
545 You Won't Find Another Fool Like Me
....Polydor 2058 421
665 Never Ending Song Of Love ......Philips 6006 125
698 Beg Steal Or Borrow ....Polydor 2058 201

ANTHONY NEWLEY
114 Why ....Decca F 11194
528 Do You Mind ....Decca F 11220

OLIVIA NEWTON-JOHN
850 Hopelessley Devoted To You..................RSO 17
*See also Olivia Newton-John and the Electric Light
Orchestra; John Travolta and Olivia Newton-John*

**OLIVIA NEWTON-JOHN AND THE ELECTRIC
LIGHT ORCHESTRA**
463 Xanadu ....Jet 185
See also Olivia Newton-John

NICOLE
521 A Little Peace ....CBS A 2365

NILSSON
58 Without You..RCA 2165

NOMAD FEATURING MC MIKEE FREEDOM
985 (I Wanna Give You) Devotion
....Rumour RUMA 25

GARY NUMAN
137 Are 'Friends' Electric ....Beggars Banquet BEG 18
555 Cars ....Beggars Banquet BEG 23
Are 'Friends' Electric credited to Tubeway Army

BILLY OCEAN
168 When The Going Gets Tough, The Tough
Get Going......................................Jive JIVE 114
879 Red Light Spells Danger ....GTO GT 85
983 Love Really Hurts Without You.......GTO GT 52

DES O'CONNOR
599 I Pretend.............................Columbia DB 8397

SINEAD O'CONNOR
151 Nothing Compares 2 U ....Ensign ENY 630

ODYSSEY
411 Use It Up And Wear It Out ....RCA PB 1962

ESTHER AND ABI OFARIM
256 Cinderella Rockefella..................Philips BF 1640

ROY ORBISON
231 Oh Pretty Woman..................London HLU 9919
380 It's Over..............................London HLU 9882
388 Only The Lonely ....London HLU 9149
796 Dream Baby..........................London HLU 9511

DONNY OSMOND
96 Puppy Love................................MGM 2006 104
210 Young Love ....MGM 2006 300
537 The Twelfth Of Never ....MGM 2006 199
See also Osmonds

LITTLE JIMMY OSMOND
86 Long Haired Lover From Liverpool
....MGM 2006 109

OSMONDS
328 Love Me For A Reason.............MGM 2006 458
694 Crazy Horses ....MGM 2006 142
755 Let Me In ....MGM 2006 321
See also Donny Osmond

GILBERT O'SULLIVAN
470 Clair..MAM 84
508 Get Down ....MAM 96

JOHNNY OTIS SHOW
664 Ma He's Making Eyes At Me
....Capitol CL 14794

OTTAWAN
706 D.I.S.C.O. ....Carrere CAR 161

OVERLANDERS
366 Michelle ....Pye 7N 17034

P

ELAINE PAIGE AND BARBARA DICKSON
125 I Know Him So Well..................RCA CHESS 3

PAPER LACE
268 Billy Don't Be A Hero..........Bus Stop BUS 1014

SIMON PARK
136 Eye Level ....Columbia DB 8946

RAY PARKER JR
718 Ghostbusters ....Arista ARIST 580

PARTNERS IN KRYME
193 Turtle Power ....Sire TURTLE 1

LUCIANO PAVAROTTI
708 Nessun Dorma...........................Decca PAV 03

FREDA PAYNE
47 Band Of Gold ....Invictus INV 502

PEPSI AND SHIRLIE
910 Heartache ....Polydor POSP 837

PET SHOP BOYS
166 Always On My Mind............Parlophone R 6171
313 It's A Sin ....Parlophone R 6158
336 Heart ....Parlophone R 6177
510 West End Girls....................Parlophone R 6115
See also Pet Shop Boys and Dusty Springfield

PET SHOP BOYS AND DUSTY SPRINGFIELD
885 What Have I Done To Deserve This
....Parlophone R 6163
See also Pet Shop Boys; Dusty Springfield

PETER AND GORDON
484 A World Without Love ....Columbia DB 7225

PETERS AND LEE
526 Welcome Home ....Philips 6006 307

265   Summer Holiday
............................Columbia DB 4977 (Shadows)
379   I Love You ....Columbia DB 4957 (Shadows)
473   Congratulations ....Columbia DB 8376
612   Saviour's Day...............................EMI XMAS 90
620   The Minute You're Gone.......Columbia DB 7496
680   Daddy's Home ....EMI 5251
692   I'm Looking Out The Window/Do You
       Wanna Dance........Columbia DB 4828 (Shadows)
693   Wind Me Up (Let Me Go) ....Columbia DB 7745
745   Voice In The Wilderness
............................Columbia DB 4398 (Shadows)
749   It's All In The Game ....Columbia DB 7089
929   The Best Of Me...............................EMI EM 78
       See also Cliff Richard and the Young Ones; Shadows

CLIFF RICHARD AND THE YOUNG ONES
310   Living Doll ....WEA YZ 65
       See also Cliff Richard

LIONEL RICHIE
52   Hello ....Motown TMG 1330
747   All Night Long (All Night) ..Motown TMG 1319

RIGHT SAID FRED
282   Deeply Dippy ....Tug SNOG 3
655   I'm Too Sexy ....Tug SNOG 1

RIGHTEOUS BROTHERS
122   Unchained Melody...........Verve/Polydor PO 101
506   You've Lost That Lovin' Feelin'
....London HLU 9943

MINNIE RIPERTON
844   Loving You ....Epic EPC 3121

B.A. ROBERTSON
959   Bang Bang..................................Asylum K 13152

SMOKEY ROBINSON
467   Being With You ....Motown TMG 1223
       See also Smokey Robinson and the Miracles

SMOKEY ROBINSON AND THE MIRACLES
529   Tears Of A Clown ....Tamla Motown TMG 745
       See also Smokey Robinson

LORD ROCKINGHAM'S XI
212   Hoots Mon ....Decca F 11059

TOMMY ROE
604   Dizzy...Stateside SS 2143

KENNY ROGERS
435   Coward Of The County ....United Artists UP 614
558   Lucille ....United Artists UP 36242
653   Ruby Don't Take Your Love To Town
....Reprise RS 20829
       Ruby Don't Take Your Love To Town *credited to*
       Kenny Rogers and the First Edition

ROLLING STONES
77   Honky Tonk Women ....Decca F 12952
334   The Last Time ....Decca F 12104
353   Get Off Of My Cloud.....................Decca F 12263
448   (I Can't Get No) Satisfaction ....Decca F 12220
452   Jumping Jack Flash ....Decca F 12782
534   It's All Over Now ....Decca F 11934
593   Paint It, Black ....Decca F 12395
647   Little Red Rooster........................Decca F 12014

716   Brown Sugar/Bitch/Let It Rock
......................................Rolling Stones RS 19100
778   Nineteenth Nervous Breakdown ...Decca F 12331

LINDA RONSTADT WITH AARON NEVILLE
876   Don't Know Much....................Elektra EKR 100

ROSE ROYCE
906   Love Don't Live Here Anymore
....Whitfield K 17236

DIANA ROSS
158   I'm Still Waiting ....Tamla Motown TMG 781
257   Chain Reaction ....Capitol CL 386
825   When You Tell Me That You Love Me
....EMI EM 217
861   Upside Down ....Motown TMG 1195

DEMIS ROUSSOS
641   The Roussos Phenomenon EP
....Philips DEMIS 001
855   When Forever Has Gone ....Philips 6042 186

ROXY MUSIC
512   Jealous Guy.......................EG/Polydor ROXY 2
703   Dance Away.............................Polydor POSP 44

**ROYAL PHILHARMONIC ORCHESTRA,
CONDUCTOR LOUIS CLARK**
809   Hooked On Classics............................RCA 109

**PIPES AND DRUMS AND MILITARY BAND OF
THE ROYAL SCOTS DRAGOON GUARDS**
76   Amazing Grace ....RCA 2191

RUBETTES
176   Sugar Baby Love ....Polydor 2058 442

JENNIFER RUSH
67   The Power Of Love ....CBS A 5003

BARRY RYAN
802   Eloise ....MGM 1442

— **S** —

S EXPRESS
475   Theme From S Express
....Rhythm King LEFT 21

SAILOR
905   Glass Of Champagne....................Epic EPC 3770

ST. WINIFRED'S SCHOOL CHOIR
438   There's No One Quite Like Grandma
....MFP FP 900

SALT-N-PEPA
732   Push It/Tramp ....Champion CHAMP 51/ffrr FFR 2
840   Let's Talk About Sex.............................ffrr F 162

MIKE SARNE WITH WENDY RICHARD
394   Come Outside ....Parlophone R 4902

PETER SARSTEDT
138   Where Do You Go To My Lovely
....United Artists UP 2262

TELLY SAVALAS
425   If...MCA 174

LEO SAYER
294   When I Need You ....Chrysalis CHS 2127

957   You Make Me Feel Like Dancing
....Chrysalis CHS 2119
993   The Show Must Go On........Chrysalis CHS 2023

SCAFFOLD
127   Lily The Pink ....Parlophone R 5734

SCORPIONS
871   Wind Of Change ....Vertigo VER 58

SEARCHERS
341   Needles And Pins..........................Pye 7N 15594
443   Sweets For My Sweet....................Pye 7N 15533
464   Don't Throw Your Love Away ....Pye 7N 15630

SEEKERS
239   The Carnival Is Over............Columbia DB 7711
420   I'll Never Find Another You ..Columbia DB 7431
673   Morningtown Ride ....Columbia DB 8060

SHADOWS
10   Wonderful Land....................Columbia DB 4790
62   Apache ....Columbia DB 4484
605   Dance On............................Columbia DB 4948
621   Foot Tapper ....Columbia DB 4984
642   Kon-Tiki ....Columbia DB 4698
826   Atlantis ....Columbia DB 7047
See also Cliff Richard

SHAGGY
376   Oh Carolina ....Greensleeves GRE 361

SHAKESPEARS SISTER
9   Stay ....London LON 314

SHAMEN
154   Ebeneezer Goode ....One Little Indian 78 TP7

SHANICE
816   I Love Your Smile ....Motown TMG 1401

DEL SHANNON
213   Runaway...............................London HLX 9317
943   Swiss Maid ....London HLX 9609

HELEN SHAPIRO
224   You Don't Know ....Columbia DB 4670
225   Walkin' Back To Happiness....Columbia DB 4715
699   Tell Me What He Said ....Columbia DB 4782

FEARGAL SHARKEY
485   A Good Heart ....Virgin VS 808

SANDIE SHAW
275   Puppet On A String......................Pye 7N 17272
337   (There's) Always Something There To Remind
Me..Pye 7N 15704
357   Long Live Love ....Pye 7N 15841

ANNE SHELTON
120   Lay Down Your Arms ....Philips PB 616

SHOWADDYWADDY
218   Under The Moon Of Love....................Bell 1495
955   Three Steps To Heaven..........................Bell 1426
976   Hey Rock And Roll..............................Bell 1357

SIMON AND GARFUNKEL
236   Bridge Over Troubled Water ....CBS 4790
See also Art Garfunkel

SIMPLE MINDS
501   Belfast Child ....Virgin SMX 3

SIMPLY RED
742   If You Don't Know Me By Now
....Elektra YZ 377
911   Holding Back The Years..............Elektra EKR 29

SIMPSONS
273   Do The Bartman ....Geffen GEF 87

FRANK SINATRA
245   Strangers In The Night.............Reprise R 23052
See also Nancy Sinatra and Frank Sinatra

NANCY SINATRA
207   These Boots Are Made For Walkin'
....Reprise R 20432
*See also Nancy Sinatra and Frank Sinatra; Nancy and
Lee*

NANCY SINATRA AND FRANK SINATRA
372   Somethin' Stupid....................Reprise RS 23166
See also Nancy Sinatra; Frank Sinatra

SINITTA
808   So Macho/Cruising......................Fanfare FAN 7

SISTER SLEDGE
132   Frankie ....Atlantic A 9547

SLADE
100   Merry Xmas Everybody............Polydor 2058 422
180   Cum On Feel The Noize ....Polydor 2058 339
182   Coz I Luv You........................Polydor 2058 155
302   Mama Weer All Crazee Now ....Polydor 2058 274
362   Skweeze Me Pleeze Me ....Polydor 2058 377
601   Take Me Bak 'Ome..................Polydor 2058 231
735   My Oh My..RCA 373
859   Far Far Away........................Polydor 2058 522
1000   My Frend Stan ....Polydor 2058 407

PERCY SLEDGE
900   When A Man Loves A Woman ...Atlantic 584 001

SL2
704   On A Ragga Tip ....XL XLS 29

SLIK
543   Forever And Ever ....Bell 1464

SMALL FACES
580   All Or Nothing............................Decca F 12470

SMART E'S
998   Sesame's Treet ....Suburban Base SUBBASE 12S

O.C. SMITH
774   Son Of Hickory Holler's Tramp ....CBS 3343

SNAP!
30   Rhythm Is A Dancer ....Arista 115309
454   The Power....................................Arista 113133
762   Exterminate! ....Arista 74321106967
Exterminate! features Niki Haris

SNOW
701   Informer ....East West America A 8436

SOFT CELL
386   Tainted Love ....Some Bizzare BZS 2
963   Torch ....Some Bizzare BZS 9

SONIA
460   You'll Never Stop Me Loving You
....Chrysalis CHS 3385

SONNY AND CHER
415 I Got You Babe ....Atlantic AT 4035
     See also Cher

DAVID SOUL
147 Don't Give Up On Us ....Private Stock PVT 84
277 Silver Lady.........................Private Stock PVT 115
764 Going In With My Eyes Open
     ....Private Stock PVT 99

SOUL II SOUL FEATURING CARON WHEELER
186 Back To Life (However Do You Want Me)
     ....10 TEN 265

SPACE
727 Magic Fly ....Pye Int 7N 25746

SPANDAU BALLET
181 True ....Reformation SPAN 1
882 Gold......................................Reformation SPAN 2

SPARKS
848 This Town Ain't Big Enough For Both Of Us
     ....Island WIP 6193

SPECIALS
261 Ghost Town ....2 Tone CHSTT 17
492 Too Much Too Young (EP) ......2 Tone CHSTT 7
     Billed as Special AKA featuring Rico on Too Much
     Too Young EP

SPITTING IMAGE
358 The Chicken Song ....Virgin SPIT 1

DUSTY SPRINGFIELD
636 You Don't Have To Say You Love Me
     ....Philips BF 1482
     See also Pet Shop Boys and Dusty Springfield

LISA STANSFIELD
449 All Around The World....................Arista 112693

ALVIN STARDUST
574 Jealous Mind...............................Magnet MAG 5

KAY STARR
546 Rock And Roll Waltz..................HMV POP 168

RINGO STARR
851 Back Off Boogaloo.........................Apple R 5944

STARSHIP
145 Nothing's Gonna Stop Us Now ..Grunt FB 49757

STARSOUND
908 Stars On 45 Vol 2 ....CBS A 1407
939 Stars On 45 ....CBS 1102

STATUS QUO
648 Down Down ....Vertigo 6059 114
903 What You're Proposin'.................Vertigo QUO 3

TOMMY STEELE
634 Singing The Blues.........................Decca F 10819

CAT STEVENS
868 Matthew And Son ....Deram DM 110

RAY STEVENS
623 The Streak ....Janus 6146 201
737 Bridget The Midget (The Queen Of The Blues)
     ....CBS 7070

SHAKIN' STEVENS
206 Green Door ....Epic A 1354
247 This Ole House...........................Epic EPC 9555
482 Merry Christmas Everyone ....Epic A 6769
614 Oh Julie..................................Epic EPC A 1742
679 You Drive Me Crazy.......................Epic A 1165
878 A Love Worth Waiting For...............Epic A 4291
916 The Shakin' Stevens EP...............Epic SHAKY 1

DAVE STEWART WITH BARBARA GASKIN
209 It's My Party ....Broken BROKEN 2

JERMAINE STEWART
814 We Don't Have To...........................10 TEN 96

ROD STEWART
60   Maggie May ....Mercury 6052 097
109 Sailing ....Warner Bros. K 16600
128 I Don't Want To Talk About It/First Cut Is
     The Deepest ....Riva 7
299 Baby Jane ....Warner Bros. W 9608
539 You Wear It Well....................Mercury 6052 171
624 Da Ya Think I'm Sexy ....Riva 17

STRANGLERS
835 Golden Brown..............................Liberty BP 407

STRAWBS
722 Part Of The Union ....A&M AMS 7047

BARBRA STREISAND
298 Woman In Love ....CBS 8966

STYLISTICS
280 Can't Give You Anything (But My Love)
     ....Avco 6105 039
989 You Make Me Feel Brand New ....Avco 6105 028

DONNA SUMMER
185 I Feel Love ....GTO GT 100

SUPREMES
517 Baby Love ....Stateside SS 350

SURVIVOR
129 Eye Of The Tiger ....Scotti Bros. SCTA 2411

SWEET
82   Blockbuster..................................RCA 2305
738 Ballroom Blitz ....RCA 2043
754 Hell Raiser ....RCA 2357
760 Teenage Rampage ....RCA LPBO 5005
805 Co-Co...RCA 2087
870 Fox On The Run ....RCA 2524

SWEET SENSATION
645 Sad Sweet Dreamer ....Pye 7N 45385

SWINGING BLUE JEANS
936 Hippy Hippy Shake ....HMV POP 1242

────────── **T** ──────────

T. REX
45   Hot Love ....Fly BUG 6
165 Metal Guru...............................EMI MARC 1
188 Get It On...Fly BUG 10
413 Telegram Sam ....T Rex 101
658 Jeepster ....Fly BUG 16
770 Children Of The Revolution ....EMI MARC 2
946 Solid Gold Easy Action ....EMI MARC 3

TAKE THAT
931   Why Can't I Wake Up With You
....RCA 74321133107

TAMS
237   Hey Girl Don't Bother Me ....Probe PRO 532

R. DEAN TAYLOR
958   Indiana Wants Me ....Tamla Motown TMG 763

TEARS FOR FEARS
797   Everybody Wants To Rule The World
....Mercury IDEA 9

TECHNOTRONIC
803   Get Up (Before The Night Is Over)
....Swanyard SYR 8
828   Pump Up The Jam....................Swanyard SYR 4
Get Up *features Ya Kid K,* Pump Up The Jam
features Felly

TEDDY BEARS
888   To Know Him Is To Love Him
....London HL 8733

TEENAGERS FEATURING FRANKIE LYMON
219   Why Do Fools Fall In Love....Columbia DB 3772

TEMPERANCE SEVEN
564   You're Driving Me Crazy.......Parlophone R 4757

TEMPTATIONS
811   My Girl ....Epic 6576767

10 C.C.
458   I'm Not In Love ....Mercury 6008 014
567   Rubber Bullets ....UK 36
584   Dreadlock Holiday ....Mercury 6008 035
820   Donna...UK 6

JOE TEX
984   Ain't Gonna Bump No More (With No Big Fat
Woman) ....Epic EPC 5035

THREE DEGREES
395   When Will I See You Again
....................................Philadelphia Int PIR 2155

THUNDERCLAP NEWMAN
355   Something In The Air...................Track 604 031

TIFFANY
296   I Think We're Alone Now........MCA MCA 1211

TIGHT FIT
264   The Lion Sleeps Tonight ....Jive JIVE 9

JOHNNY TILLOTSON
442   Poetry In Motion ....London HLA 9231

TIMELORDS
637   Doctorin' The Tardis......................KLF KLF 003

TORNADOS
95   Telstar ....Decca F 11494

T'PAU
104   China In Your Hand ....Siren SRN 64

TRAFFIC
980   Hole In My Shoe ....Island WIP 6017

JOHN TRAVOLTA
970   Sandy ....Polydor POSP 6
See also John Travolta and Olivia Newton-John

JOHN TRAVOLTA AND OLIVIA NEWTON-JOHN
4   You're The One That I Want ....RSO 006
21   Summer Nights.....................................RSO 18
See also John Travolta; Olivia Newton-John

TREMELOES
306   Silence Is Golden ....CBS 2723
834   (Call Me) Number One ....CBS 4582
See also Brian Poole and the Tremeloes

JACKIE TRENT
595   Where Are You Now (My Love)....Pye 7N 15776

TROGGS
446   With A Girl Like You.................Fontana TF 717

TWEETS
860   The Birdie Song (Birdie Dance)........PRT 7P 219

CONWAY TWITTY
61   It's Only Make Believe ....MGM 992

2 UNLIMITED
66   No Limit ....PWL Continental PWL 256
788   Get Ready For This..PWL Continental PWL 206

BONNIE TYLER
410   Total Eclipse Of The Heart ....CBS TYLER 1
776   Holding Out For A Hero ....CBS A 4251

TYMES
635   Ms Grace ....RCA 2493

TYPICALLY TROPICAL
535   Barbados.......................................Gull GULS 14

U

UB40
249   Red Red Wine.........................DEP Int 7DEP 7
554   I Got You Babe.......................DEP Int 7DEP 20
I Got You Babe features Chrissie Hynde

TRACEY ULLMAN
869   They Don't Know..........................Stiff BUY 180

ULTRAVOX
672   Vienna ....Chrysalis CHS 2481

UNDERCOVER
934   Baker Street............................PWL Int PWL 239

UNION GAP FEATURING GARY PUCKETT
124   Young Girl ....CBS 3365

UNIT FOUR PLUS TWO
587   Concrete And Clay ....Decca F 12071

MIDGE URE
588   If I Was ....Chrysalis URE 1

USA FOR AFRICA
495   We Are The World ....CBS USAID 1

U2
631   Desire ....Island IS 400
639   The Fly ....Island IS 500

V

RICKY VALANCE
285   Tell Laura I Love Her.............Columbia DB 4493

DICKIE VALENTINE
325   Christmas Alphabet......................Decca F 10628

LUTHER VANDROSS AND JANET JACKSON
893   The Best Things In Life Are Free
      ....Perspective PERSS 7400

VANILLA ICE
121   Ice Ice Baby ....SBK SBK 18

VARIOUS ARTISTS
930   The Brits 1990 ....RCA PB 43565

FRANKIE VAUGHAN
123   Garden Of Eden............................Philips PB 660
263   Tower Of Strength.......................Philips PB 1195
686   Green Door..................................Philips PB 640

VILLAGE PEOPLE
221   Y.M.C.A. ....Mercury 6007 192
917   In The Navy ....Mercury 6007 209

W

WALKER BROTHERS
179   The Sun Ain't Gonna Shine Anymore
      ....Philips BF 1473
600   Make It Easy On Yourself ....Philips BF 1428

ANITA WARD
462   Ring My Bell ....TK TKR 7543

DIONNE WARWICK
865   Heartbreaker............................Arista ARIST 496

KEITH WEST
887   Excerpt From 'A Teenage Opera'
      ....Parlophone R 5623

WET WET WET
156   Goodnight Girl......................Precious JEWEL 17
196   With A Little Help From My Friends
      ....Childline CHILD 1

WHAM!
289   Freedom ....Epic A 4743
421   Wake Me Up Before You Go-Go .....Epic A 4440
424   I'm Your Man....................................Epic A 6716
432   The Edge Of Heaven/Where Did Your Heart Go
      ....Epic FIN 1
663   Last Christmas/Everything She Wants ....Epic A 4949
853   Bad Boys ....Innervision A 3143

BARRY WHITE
450   You're The First The Last My Everything
      ....20th Century BTC 2133
896   You See The Trouble With Me
      ....20th Century BTC 2277

ROGER WHITTAKER
937   The Last Farewell ....EMI 2294

WHO
852   My Generation........................Brunswick 05944
982   I'm A Boy ....Reaction 591 004

KIM WILDE
837   Kids In America....................................RAK 327
877   You Keep Me Hangin' On ....MCA KIM 4

MARTY WILDE
793   A Teenager In Love ....Philips PB 926

ANDY WILLIAMS
375   Butterfly................................London HLA 8399
768   Almost There ....CBS 201813

DANNY WILLIAMS
399   Moon River ....HMV POP 932

DENIECE WILLIAMS
455   Free..CBS 4978
884   Let's Hear It For The Boy.................CBS A 4319

BRUCE WILLIS
799   Under The Boardwalk ....Motown ZB 41349

JACKIE WILSON
134   Reet Petite ....Coral Q 72290

WIZZARD
191   See My Baby Jive ....Harvest HAR 5070
611   Angel Fingers.........................Harvest HAR 5076

STEVIE WONDER
32   I Just Called To Say I Love You
      ....Motown TMG 1349

WURZELS
412   Combine Harvester (Brand New Key)..EMI 2450

TAMMY WYNETTE
295   Stand By Your Man.....................Epic EPC 7137
      See also KLF

Y

YARDBIRDS
759   Heart Full Of Soul................Columbia DB 7594

YAZZ AND THE PLASTIC POPULATION
98   The Only Way Is Up....................Big Life BLR 4

PAUL YOUNG
252   Wherever I Lay My Hat (That's My Home)
      ....CBS A 3371
709   Love Of The Common People ....CBS A 3585

Z

ZAGER AND EVANS
344   In The Year 2525 (Exordium and Terminus)
      ....RCA 1860